THE DRUM MAJOR INSTINCT

THE DRUM MAJOR INSTINCT
MARTIN LUTHER KING JR.'S THEORY OF POLITICAL SERVICE

JUSTIN ROSE

THE UNIVERSITY OF GEORGIA PRESS ATHENS

A Sarah Mills Hodge Fund Publication
This publication is made possible in part through a grant from the Hodge
Foundation in memory of its founder, Sarah Mills Hodge, who devoted her
life to the relief and education of African Americans in Savannah, Georgia.

Set in 9.5/14 Utopia Std by Kaelin Chappell Broaddus

Most University of Georgia Press titles are
available from popular e-book vendors.

Printed digitally

Library of Congress Cataloging-in-Publication Data

Names: Rose, Justin, 1982- author.
Title: The drum major instinct : Martin Luther King Jr.'s theory of political
    service / Justin Rose.
Description: Athens : The University of Georgia Press, [2019] | Series: The
    Morehouse College King Collection series on civil & human rights |
    Includes bibliographical references and index.
Identifiers: LCCN 2018054026| ISBN 9780820355528 (hardcover : alk. paper) |
    ISBN 9780820355542 (pbk. : alk. paper) | ISBN 9780820355535 (ebook)
Subjects: LCSH: King, Martin Luther, Jr., 1929-1968—Political and social views.
    | Social action—United States—History—20th century.
Classification: LCC E185.97.K5 R5978 2019 | DDC 323.092 [B] —dc23

    LC record available at https://lccn.loc.gov/2018054026

Dedicated to the loving memory of
Hannah Teklemariam

CONTENTS

ACKNOWLEDGMENTS

This book feels as if it were a lifetime in the making. Consequently, it will be impossible to thank all the people who deserve credit for some aspect of this project. However, I must begin by thanking Lawrie Balfour, Melvin Rogers, Stephen K. White, and Claudrena Harold for their mentorship and belief in this project.

Along the way, this project has benefited from great colleagues who have aided my project tremendously. This list includes but is not limited to Greta Snydor, William Umphres, John Thabiti Willis, Kim Gallon, Rodmon King, Khuram Hussain, Ervin Kosta, James McCorkle, Kevin Dunn, Susan Brewer-Osorio, Cedric Johnson, Heather May, Tremayne Robertson, Renee Grant, Tiffany Barber, Ed Brockenbrough, Sheldon Fields (and household), and all my great colleagues in the Department of Political Science and the Africana Studies Program at Hobart and William Smith Colleges (HWS).

I am also extremely grateful for the Jefferson Scholars Foundation of the University of Virginia for helping to fund the early years of my research. This project also benefitted from the leadership and funding provided by Provost Titilayo Ufomata at HWS. Finally, I thank the Center for Teaching and Learning at HWS for sponsoring retreats that have greatly aided the writing of this project.

Special thanks to Vicki Crawford, Walter Biggins, the entire staff of the University of Georgia Press, and my reviewers.

Last, but certainly not least, I want to give a heartfelt thanks to my closest friends and family who have provided encouragement and faith at every step of this process. Although there are too many to name, I need to single out Lynne Magruder, Hassan Assad, and Brad Burke for special recognition.

Ultimately, this book would not be a reality without three individuals, above all else. First, and foremost, is my good friend and colleague Andrew Douglas. I am forever indebted for his friendship and countless hours reading and conversing about my project. Thank you! Finally, I want to acknowledge the tremendous sacrifice, unconditional love, and incessant support of Solomé and Miles Rose. You two are truly the salt of the earth.

THE DRUM MAJOR INSTINCT

INTRODUCTION
THE DRUM MAJOR INSTINCT

Jesus gave us a new norm of greatness. If you want to be important—wonderful. If you want to be recognized—wonderful. If you want to be great—wonderful. But recognize that he who is greatest among you shall be your servant.
—MARTIN LUTHER KING JR.

On a serene Sunday in October 2011, the Martin Luther King, Jr. Memorial was officially dedicated on the National Mall. Although the newly erected monument made King the first black American and nonpresident to be granted such an honor, it was not without its critics. Specifically, Maya Angelou, who was one of the consultants for the memorial, took issue with an inscription etched into the north side of the towering statue that read, "I was a drum major for justice, peace and righteousness." Rather than directly quoting King, the statement paraphrased a section of King's 1968 "The Drum Major Instinct" sermon. In the actual quotation King (1986) said, "If you want to say that I was a drum major, say that I was a drum major for justice. Say that I was a drum major for peace. I was a drum major for righteousness" (267). According to Angelou, "[King] had a humility that comes from deep inside. The 'if' clause that is left out is salient. Leaving it out changes the meaning completely." Rather than honoring King's deeply held commitments, Angelou charged that the monument made him "look like an arrogant twit" (Weingarten and Ruane 2011). Others agreed, and, bowing to growing criticism, the Department of the Interior decided to remove the quotation altogether.

The profound irony of the monument's self-aggrandizing inscription is that King's sermon was not an exercise in self-glorification; rather, he sought to minimize the impulse to achieve individual distinction at the expense of others by promoting an other-oriented form of service. King did so by drawing on a biblical story in which two of Jesus's disciples—James and John—sought to distinguish themselves from the other disciples by sitting immediately beside Jesus in his kingdom. King (1986) highlighted James's and John's desire for special recognition because he believed that all humans possess this very same drive "to surpass others, to achieve distinction, to lead the parade" (260). King labeled this desire the drum major instinct since drum majors have the singular privilege of strutting at the head of marching bands. King cautioned, though, if the drive for individual distinction is left unchecked, it will eventually lead to "snobbish exclusivism" and a hypercompetitiveness that will cause a man "to push others down in order to push himself up" (262). Ultimately, King argued that the unfettered drum major instinct has inflicted American society in the form of the triple evils, which he identified as pathological racism, excessive materialism, and destructive militarism (250).[1]

Even though King had misgivings about the drum major instinct, he also believed that, when it is properly channeled, the drive for greatness is a useful trait for Americans to possess. For King (1986), the most important aspect of Jesus's response to James and John was that Jesus did not chastise them for their naked ambition; instead, he "reordered priorities" (265). King said, "Jesus gave us a new norm of greatness. If you want to be important—wonderful. If you want to be recognized—wonderful. If you want to be great—wonderful. But recognize that he who is greatest among you shall be your servant" (265). According to King, Jesus taught that the drive to be great is an admirable instinct when greatness is evaluated by how much one serves others. Armed with Jesus's precept, King called on congregants at his Ebenezer Baptist Church to redefine greatness by becoming drum majors in the quest for justice, peace, and righteousness.

Throughout King's tenure in the American civil rights movement he worked to channel black Americans' drum major instincts into a form of service aimed at improving the lots of others. For instance, in King's final speech he chastised certain black, Christian ministers for not being "concerned about anything but themselves." King warned, "It's all right to talk about 'long white robes over yonder,' in all of its symbolism. But ultimately people want some suits and dresses and shoes to wear down here! It's all right to talk about 'streets flowing with milk and honey,' but God has commanded us to be concerned about the slums down here, and his children who can't eat three square meals a day" (King 1986, 282). Just as Jesus reordered the priorities of James and John in their quest to achieve distinction, King argued that ascension to heaven began with descension into America's ghettos. Thus, within King's theoretical framework the Christian notion of service was transformed into a radical political concept aimed at transforming the structures and values of American society.

Admittedly, the term "radical" is fraught and highly subjective. However, when I refer to King's theory of political service as radical, I mean to convey that it does what Ella Baker described as "getting down to and understanding the root cause" (qtd. in Ransby 2003, 1). In this sense, King's political project can be aptly described as an incessant excavation of the roots of the triple evils in American society. Near the end of King's life he confessed, "I have found out that all that I have been doing in trying to correct this system in America has been in vain.... I am trying to get to the roots of it to see just what ought to be done.... The whole thing will have to be done away" (Garrow 2004, 580). King believed that America could only be cured of the triple evils by undergoing a radical restructuring of society. Unfortunately, King's life would be taken on the balcony of the Lorraine Motel before he could complete his life's work of fomenting a revolutionary spirit of service among his fellow citizens.

Since King's death the radical dimensions of his commitment to service, like the fate of the quotation etched into the north side of the national monument, have been altered and erased from his legacy. For example, in 1994 King's commitment to a radical form of service was seemingly apotheosized within American society when the U.S. federal government transformed the Martin Luther King Jr. federal holiday into a national day of service. With the passage of the Martin Luther King, Jr. Federal Holiday and Service Act, the King holiday, according to the Corporation for National and Community Service, was meant to become a call "for Americans from all walks of life to work together to provide solutions to our most pressing national problems" (The Official MLK Day of Service Site). However, rather than engaging in a form of service that collectively resists the triple evils of American society, as King conceived of service, Americans are encouraged to honor his legacy by participating in an apolitical and voluntary action, such as cleaning up a local playground or serving a meal at a soup kitchen.[2] In this sense, King's theory of political service—one that calls for the transformation of self, others, and unjust structures—has been replaced with a neoliberal conception of service—one that is a private, individualized, and supererogatory activity that merely promotes doing good deeds while leaving structures of injustice wholly intact (Barber 1992).

What the row over the national monument and the apolitical celebration of the King holiday illustrate is the nation's continual veneration of a deradicalized mythos of King. These ritualistic celebrations have transformed King into what Kevin Bruyneel (2014) calls a "haloed myth." According to Bruyneel, within American politics King has come to symbolize a "post-racial society in which collective and structural concerns about racial equality have been displaced by neoliberal governing priorities that emphasize privatization, economic efficiency, profit and liberal individualism" (76–77). Similarly, Nikhil Pal Singh (2004, 13) charges that King has been mythologized as a "redemptive national icon" who represents America's triumph over the triple evils. Additionally, Eddie Glaude (2016) claims that the purposeful transmogrification of King, by leading political figures from the left and the right, into a heroic symbol of American racial justice has caused King's radical commitments to be disremembered. Glaude's point is that King is useful within the contemporary political context insomuch as his biting critiques of American "white supremacy, poverty, and empire" are actively forgotten (103).[3] These scholars all point to the way in which King's legacy is purposely deployed to promote the neoliberal idea that America has overcome its struggles with racism, poverty, and militarism, thereby discouraging contemporary Americans from engaging in the work necessary to combat these forms of structural injustice.

In recent years, a rich stream of scholarship (Harding 1996; Dyson 2000; Dawson 2001; Kelley 2002; Singh 2004; Glaude 2016) has worked to reclaim the radical dimensions of King's legacy. However, much of the scholarship on the "radical King" portrays him as a modern-day American prophet who was a gifted rhetorician and activist who spoke truth to power (Chappell 2004; Howard-Pitney 2005; Shulman 2008; West 2015). According to Lester Spence (2015), the limits of turning to a prophetic version of King—even a radicalized version—is that 1960s prophetic utterance does very little to actually galvanize contemporary Americans to do the work necessary to address neoliberal forms of structural injustice. Interestingly, Spence's concerns are not altogether different from those of scholars who express wariness about the sanitization of King's legacy. This is because Spence is also deeply troubled by the dangers that a mythological representation of King's legacy presents to collective action. Spence cautions, "Freezing both King and the Civil Rights Movement demobilizes black communities by creating a historically inaccurate standard, a perfect standard they cannot possibly hope to meet, a perfect standard the people they are being compared to themselves didn't meet" (110). As a result, Spence suggests that we "do ourselves a service by leaving prophets, even ones like King, and public intellectuals in the past" (111).

Collectively, these scholars highlight the danger of portraying King as either a deradicalized civil rights advocate or a radical prophet whose reliance on gifted rhetoric is out of step with the need for concerted efforts aimed at combatting the unique challenges of our contemporary neoliberal political moment. More specifically, contemporary scholars are increasingly concerned about how the "neoliberal racial order" suppresses collective action aimed at challenging unjust economic and political structures since the ideology "provides individualist-grounded, competition-driven, market values for attacks on mass politics, notions of solidarity and cooperation, and collective mutual responsibility" (Dawson and Francis 2016, 42). I share similar concerns about how the mythologizing of King's legacy has the effect of stymying collective political action in our contemporary neoliberal moment. However, instead of leaving King in the past, I believe that it is more important than ever that we explore King's political thought. Although several book-length manuscripts by theologians have systematically explored various aspects of King's thought (Cone 1991; Ivory 1997; Wills 2011; Burrow 2014), he has not received the same in-depth explication as a uniquely political thinker.[4] By engaging King as a political thinker, I will go beyond revealing a radical dimension of his activism or highlighting his rare ability to eloquently and powerfully speak truth to power. Ultimately, I rediscover one of King's most celebrated and yet most underappreciated contributions to political praxis—his theory of political service.

Despite the importance that King placed on service in his personal life and political ruminations, he never explicitly defined the concept. Furthermore, there has been no comprehensive study of how King politicized the Christian conception of service and how, if at all, it is linked to social justice within his overall theoretical framework. Toward this end, I draw on King's sermons, political speeches, and writings to construct his theory of political service.

King's theory of political service has three central components. First, King (1986) began with a configuration of humanity, which posited that all of humanity is tied into an "inescapable network of mutuality" such that no member of society can fully flourish if there are structural barriers preventing others from flourishing (290). Second, having acknowledged the existence of structural injustice, King's theory of political service required that Americans cultivate a sense of love and concern for their fellow members of society, which would motivate them to work collectively toward transforming others and structures of injustice. Finally, King contended that all members of society have the responsibility to participate in collective forms of resistance. This meant that even the oppressed were obligated to engage in political service. Therefore, marginalized peoples' struggles against injustice were considered an essential aspect of service. Taken together, King's theory of political service calls on all Americans, but especially black Americans, to engage in other-centered, collective action aimed at transforming themselves, others, and structures of injustice.

King's emphasis on the role of black Americans in his theory of political service stands in sharp contrast to the view held by many, including some of his supporters. As the democratic thinker, activist, and former special assistant to King, Harry Boyte (2004), explains, "An etymology of service illustrates the problem. Service is from the Latin *servus*, meaning slave, associated with 'servile' and 'serf.' In one of its meanings, 'performing duties connected with a position,' service is a useful bridge for reconnecting with the world. Yet in all meanings, service is associated with other-directedness. The service giver, in focusing on the needs of those being served, adopts a stance of selflessness or disinterestedness. Service is the paradigmatic stance of the outside expert. But interests and people working to further their interests are the elemental particles of politics" (12). Boyte's attribution of service to the role of the outside expert points to the widely held neoliberal belief that service is an activity solely performed by the privileged—in both knowledge and positionality. However, this conception of service is needlessly limited. As Benjamin Barber (1992) observes, "Service to the neighborhood and to the nation are not the gift of altruists but a duty of free men and women whose freedom is itself wholly dependent on the assumption of political responsibilities" (246). Likewise, King argued that despite being systematically oppressed, black Americans still bore a political responsibility to serve their nation by engaging in the struggle for justice.

The irony of inverting the roles of the privileged experts and the oppressed freedom fighters was not lost on King. As he noted, "It is a paradox that those Negroes who have given up on America are doing more to improve it than are its professional patriots" (King 1986, 327). Despite this burdensome reality, King maintained that "the black revolution is much more than a struggle for the rights of Negroes." Instead, King argued that it is better understood as a form of political service to the nation, which "is forcing America to face all its interrelated flaws—racism, poverty, militarism and materialism. It is exposing evils that are rooted deeply in the whole structure of our society. It reveals systemic rather than superficial flaws and suggests that radical reconstruction of society itself is the real issue to be faced" (315). Therefore, King believed that "Americans who genuinely treasure our national ideals . . . should welcome the stirring of Negro demands" because the black revolution had the potential to "catalyze the drastic reforms that will save us from social catastrophe" (315).

By casting black Americans as the protagonists in the battle to redeem the soul of America, I read King within at least one strain of the black radical tradition. I have in mind what Cedric Robinson (1983) and Anthony Bogues (2006) consider a core feature of black radical thought, which is the "quest for a new definition of the human being" (Bogues 2006, 419). According to King (1986), the black American struggle had exposed the need for America to undergo "a radical revolution of values" (240). King charged that the values embraced by many Americans reflected the fact that they configured humanity in a manner that does not recognize the dignity and respect of all. Thus, America needed to "shift from a thing-oriented to a person-oriented society." As King explained, "When machines and computers, profit motives and property rights, are considered more important than people, the giant triplets of racism, extreme materialism, and militarism are incapable of being conquered" (240). Understood within this context, we can see what was at stake in King's "The Drum Major Instinct" sermon. King firmly believed that the impulse to define one's greatness in terms of achieving individual distinction at the expense of others was a direct reflection of how society configured and assigned value to humanity. Therefore, King read Jesus's extolment of service as the ultimate measure of greatness to be a directive to reconfigure humanity in a manner that assigns value to collective action aimed at transforming self, others, and structures of injustice.

It may be tempting to dismiss King's concerns about the configuration of humanity as too abstract to be relevant to the political struggle of our contemporary moment. However, this would be a grave mistake. As Keeanga-Yamahtta Taylor (2016) notes, within many of King's pronouncements "are painful continuities between the present and the past that remind us that, in some cases, the past is not yet the past" (2). In our contemporary moment we hear echoes of King's warnings about the drum major instinct in the words of scholars who express concern about the way in which humanity is configured within neoliberalism

(Harvey 2005; Brown 2015; Spence 2015; Dawson and Francis 2016). For example, according to Wendy Brown (2015), "neoliberal rationality disseminates the *model of the market* to all domains and activities—even where money is not at issue—and configures human beings exhaustively as market actors, always, only, and everywhere as *homo oeconomicus*" (31; emphasis original). By configuring humanity in strictly economic terms, the neoliberal rationality assigns value to humans based on how well they conform to the dictates of the marketplace. Meanwhile, the marketplace demands that individuals succeed by investing in their own human capital with the aim of gaining a competitive advantage over others. Thus, neoliberalism attributes disparities between racial groups in areas such as wealth, health, and education to the failure of individuals to invest in the development of their marketable skills rather than to any form of structural injustice. The denial of structural injustice, in turn, means that the neoliberal conception of humanity actively works to suppress collective action aimed at challenging unjust economic and political structures.

Contradistinctively, King's theory of political service promotes a configuration of humanity that places value on being other-oriented instead of being self-centered and encourages cooperation within society instead of competition. By redefining humanity over and against the predominant values of neoliberalism, my claim is that King provides a foundation on which a form of black radical politics can emerge in our contemporary neoliberal moment.

I flesh out the connection between King's conception of humanity and his theory of political service in the first chapter. By extensively analyzing his most oft-preached sermon, "The Three Dimensions of a Complete Life," I show how King conceptualized political service as a component necessary for human flourishing. This is because King (1986) argues that all members of human society are caught up in what he calls an "inescapable network of mutuality" (290). The inescapable network of mutuality is synonymous with the structures of injustice that burden some members of society while providing unjust benefits to others. Therefore, King implores Americans to cultivate a sense of love and concern for their fellow human beings that will, in turn, motivate them to work collectively toward transforming themselves and others but also to transform structures of injustice. Finally, King contends that all members of society have the responsibility to participate in collective forms of resistance, which means that even the oppressed are obligated to engage in political service. As aforementioned, these three claims are the central components of King's theory of political service.

Although I focus on King's attempts to get black Americans to engage in political service, he was also very much concerned with the fate of white Americans. Thus, after constructing King's theory of political service, I contrast his views on the topics of transforming white Americans and integration with the views of two of his contemporaries, Kwame Ture (Stokely Carmichael) and Charles V. Hamilton. As two of the foremost proponents of Black Power, Ture and Hamilton prove to be valuable interlocutors in terms of drawing out the subtle ways King's views on the transformation of white Americans and integration changed over time.

Despite King's many radical pronouncements, there is no gainsaying the fact that his radical legacy is repeatedly co-opted to promote race-blind, neoliberal political ends. In the second chapter, I explain how King's radical legacy lends itself to easy co-optation, in part because he often invoked the American dream when articulating his vision of a future American society. Given the contemporary understanding of the American dream as an individualistic and color-blind ideology, King's use of the American dream is repeatedly cited by conservatives seeking to push a neoliberal agenda. However, rather than viewing the American dream as an uncritical appeal to the status quo, I argue that King incorporated it into his theory of political service as a means to reshape American society. For King, the American dream represented a more inclusive America in which the universal principles of liberty, equality, and the recognition of the dignity and worth of all human beings could *only* come about through self-transformation, other-transformation, and collective action aimed at transforming structures of injustice. By revisiting King's conception and use of the American dream, I intend to not only challenge attempts to divorce King's legacy from collective action and structural change but also to restore the radical possibilities of the American dream.

Although King sought to radically reinterpret the symbol of the American dream, I am not suggesting that he was oblivious to the American nightmare. In the third chapter I discuss King alongside Ta-Nehisi Coates (2015), who, in his book *Between the World and Me*, largely defines the black American experience in terms of subjection to systematic white racial violence. By placing King into conversation with Coates, I argue that it is important to acknowledge not only the history of systemic white racial violence but also the rich tradition of gallant black Americans who preserved their sense of hope in the face of some of the bleakest expressions of the American nightmare. By exploring King's response in the immediate aftermath of the 16th Street Baptist Church bombing, I explain how he sought to encourage the black community of Birmingham to draw on whatever resources necessary to remain hopeful so as not to lose their sense of political agency. For King, the black community's ability to "go on in spite of all" was an essential aspect of his theory of political service.

In the final chapter I turn to King's thoughts on *how* to politically serve others. In other words, King believed that it was possible to cause great harm if one did not properly engage in political service. King was particularly concerned that without embracing one's own fallibility individuals would approach political service with a messianic faith that disregards others' opinions and capabilities. By examining key moments in King's life, I demonstrate how he sought to cultivate a sense of compassionate humility, which he hoped would create a space for listening to others, acceptance of one's shortcomings, and ultimately a change in one's thoughts and actions. For King, the cultivation of these sensibilities and practices were a necessary component of political service, for it helps to ensure that we can serve in a manner that is respectful and sensitive to the opinions and abilities of others, rather than replicating domineering power dynamics.

Before executing my argument, I should note that I begin with the belief that many of King's thoughts about service can be found in his early writings and sermons. As a Baptist preacher and a public speaker who had sermons and speeches that he would preach repeatedly, King provides scholars with a unique opportunity to chart the development of his thoughts by examining the changes in specific sermons and speeches over time. Consequently, in the first two chapters I isolate the sermons "The Three Dimensions of a Complete Life" and "The American Dream," respectively, for the purpose of explaining how King's views on service developed over the course of his life. Most chapters also rely heavily on King's final book-length manuscript, *Where Do We Go from Here*. I believe that this text, along with some of King's later speeches, provides us with his most mature thoughts on service. Ultimately, it is my contention that by fully exploring King's thoughts on service we will more accurately honor his legacy. More important, though, I believe that by conceiving of service as a political concept that is concerned with transforming self, others, and structures of injustice we will also gain an invaluable resource in our contemporary struggle to create a more just and democratic society.

CHAPTER 1
SERVICE AS THE NEW NORM OF GREATNESS

I'd like somebody to mention that day that Martin Luther King, Jr., tried to give his life serving others . . . I want you to say that I tried to love and serve humanity.
—MARTIN LUTHER KING JR.

I

On February 4, 1968, Martin Luther King Jr. stood in the pulpit of Ebenezer Baptist Church and preached his final sermon before his home church—"The Drum Major Instinct." Ominously, King (1986) admitted that he occasionally thought about "life's final common denominator—that something we call death" (266). King, sensing that his days were numbered, went on to soberly dictate how he wished to be memorialized at the time of his death. He specifically forbade those who survived him from mentioning his Nobel Peace Prize or other superficial markers of success. Instead, he instructed those in attendance to only highlight the one thing he viewed as his singular accomplishment: "I'd like somebody to mention that day that Martin Luther King, Jr., tried to give his life serving others . . . I want you to say that I tried to love and serve humanity" (267). Exactly two months later, King would be struck down by an assassin's bullet. At King's funeral a portion of his self-eulogizing sermon was played, thereby ensuring that his request was met. If King's aim was to be remembered for his commitment to serving others, then, in many ways, he was ultimately successful. Maybe too successful.

Fifty years to the day that King asked to be memorialized for his commitment to serving others, his message would reach one of its widest

transform self, others and structure of injustice

audiences ever. During the live airing of the National Football League's Super Bowl LII viewers were unexpectedly admonished by King to define greatness in terms of service to others. However, unlike his funeral, where his "The Drum Major Instinct" sermon was set against the backdrop of wailing mourners, this time his words provided the soundtrack for a Dodge Ram truck commercial. Predictably, the advertisement was swiftly rebuked for its use of the civil rights icon's voice to hawk automobiles. A spokesperson for the King estate offered the following explanation for their decision to green-light the project: "We found that the overall message of the ad embodied Dr. King's philosophy that true greatness is achieved by serving others. Thus, we decided to be a part of Ram's 'Built To Serve' Super Bowl program" (Holmes 2018). In other words, the estate viewed the commercial as a tremendous opportunity to further King's aim of being forever remembered for his commitment to serving others.

Despite the purportedly noble aim of the King estate, many critics decried the commercial for using King's "The Drum Major Instinct" sermon to encourage conspicuous consumption—something he explicitly denounces elsewhere in the sermon. For instance, Jack Holmes (2018), a writer for *Esquire*, offers, "But King's philosophy was hardly limited to encouraging people to serve others. In fact, what he actually said was often diametrically opposed to the kind of basic materialism and Keeping Up With the Joneses energy that clings so doggedly to American capitalism." Certainly, Holmes and others are correct to point out the hypocrisy of using King to promote neoliberal, capitalistic values. However, what is missing from this analysis is the connection between King's understanding of service and his call for a revolution of American values. Undoubtedly, King's legacy has become linked to a notion of service, which promotes an individualistic, supererogatory form of volunteerism. King, though, argued that we must push beyond this basic understanding of service by subsuming the neoliberal impulse of the drum major instinct into a desire to transform self, others, and structures of injustice. In other words, contrary to Holmes's assertion, King's theory of political service was the *means* by which he sought to actively oppose unhealthy American capitalistic values, in addition to racism and militarism.

Whether viewers of the Dodge Ram commercial ultimately agree with the company's decision to use King's voice, it is important not to lose sight of the important message embedded within the advertisement. This is especially true in our current political moment. Nearly fifty years after King preached "The Drum Major Instinct," the current president of the United States successfully ran a xenophobic, misogynistic, and racist presidential campaign while promising to "make America great again." With this in mind, it is imperative that all Americans fully interrogate their definition of greatness. As King forewarned, the drum major instinct embraces a definition of greatness that promotes the values of exclusion and fierce competitiveness as a means to achieve individual distinction at the expense of others. Accordingly, Donald J. Trump's pursuit of greatness seeks to put America first by further enshrining the triple evils of racism, economic exploitation, and militarism into the fabric of American society. However, as the Dodge Ram commercial correctly—although misguidedly—highlighted, King would argue that it is incumbent on those who are truly concerned with making America great again to embrace a new norm of greatness; that is, one that defines greatness in terms of political service to others.

II

Over the course of King's thirteen-year tenure in the civil rights movement he progressively worked to foment a revolutionary spirit of service among all Americans but especially black Americans. Serving as president of the Montgomery Improvement Association (MIA) and then the Southern Christian Leadership Conference (SCLC), King crisscrossed the United States, calling on others to become creatively maladjusted to the triple evils. King was particularly concerned with how these triplets congealed to create oppressive conditions for black Americans. In 1967 King described this oppression as rendering black Americans "50 percent of a person." He explained, "Of the good things in life, the Negro has approximately one half those of whites. Of the bad things of life, he has twice those of whites." King pointed to the fact that half of black Americans "live in substandard housing" and they earn "half the income of whites." Furthermore, "There are twice as many unemployed; the rate of infant mortality among Negroes is double that of whites; and there are twice as many Negroes dying in Vietnam as whites in proportion to their size in the population" (King 1967b, 6-7). The plight of black Americans would remain dire, King (1967a) claimed, until the nation recognizes "that the problems of racial injustice and economic injustice cannot be solved without a radical redistribution of political and economic power." Thus, King charged that it is up to those who are concerned about justice to "recapture the revolutionary spirit and go out into a sometimes hostile world, declaring eternal opposition to poverty, racism and militarism."

King's call for Americans to recapture the revolutionary spirit was not a call to topple the American government. In fact, King (1968b) claimed, "The American racial revolution has been a revolution to 'get in' rather than to overthrow" (138). For King, a revolution means that the creatively maladjusted population comes together to demand "a radical restructuring of the architecture of American society" (141). King firmly believed that when members of society work collectively to challenge the giant evils, they are engaging in a form of political service to the nation, for they are not only remaking themselves and others but they are also transforming structures of injustice. In 1967 King told a raucous crowd at the National Conference for New Politics, "So we are here because we believe, we hope, we pray that something new might emerge in the political life of this nation which will produce a new man, new structures and new institutions and a new life for mankind" (King 1967a). However, as King (1968b) explained in *Where Do We Go from Here*, "for the evils of racism, poverty and militarism to die, a new set of values must be born" (142). Thus, those who possess the revolutionary spirit do not view themselves as seeking to "integrate into all the existing values of American society." Instead, they are to be "those creative dissenters who will call our beloved nation to a higher destiny, to a new plateau of compassion, to a more noble expression of humaneness" (142). Ultimately,

the revolution requires "people of goodwill" to en~
tive political service by putting "their bodies and~
in an effort to collectively resist the triple evils (~

Much to the chagrin of other black preachers, King~
tigated conservative interpretations of Christianity, which he~
with being so concerned with "a future good 'over yonder' that they co~
dition their members to adjust to the present evils 'over here'" (King
1968b, 132). In response King argued that political service is not only a
fundamental tenet of Christianity but also a necessary component for
human flourishing. King made this argument most consistently in a series of sermons entitled "The Three Dimensions of a Complete Life."
This is one of King's most enduring homilies. He preached it in 1954 as
a trial sermon for Dexter Avenue Baptist Church, and many elements of
the sermon were present in his final sermon, "I See the Promised Land,"
which was preached nearly fourteen years later. It is important to explicate King's "Dimensions" sermons, I believe, because they contain his
most pronounced and enduring articulations of how he configured humanity.

In 1954, as King stood before Dexter Avenue Baptist Church's congregation giving his trial sermon, he made the case that there are three dimensions of a complete life. He explained that a fully three-dimensional
life requires love of oneself (length) be complemented by serving others
(breadth) and searching for God (height). Piecing together the different
versions of the "Dimensions" sermons, King's theological understanding of the human being can be summed up in the following way: First, as
a Baptist minister, King began with the premise that there is a God who
created the world and all of humanity. According to King's Christian
worldview, God is the Father and all human beings are His children—
consequently, all humans are brothers and sisters. In creating humanity, though, God gave all of His children an innate desire to reach their
fullest potential. The goal of reaching one's fullest potential begins with
the pursuit of one's own ends. Yet God has structured the world, according to King, so that all of humanity is naturally interdependent and consequently one cannot reach his or her fullest potential without serving
others. Finally, in order to reach one's full potential one must also con-

ually seek God. For the purposes of this chapter I will only focus on ne first two dimensions; I will focus exclusively on the third dimension in chapter three.

King (2007) taught that the first dimension of a complete life begins with acknowledging that God, in creating humanity, has given all individuals different talents and abilities and that there is an "onward push to the end of realizing [one's] inner capacity" (399). He called this the length of life, which he viewed as the selfish dimension that displays an "inward concern for one's own welfare" (397). King was not suggesting that there was anything inherently wrong with this selfishness. In fact, he acknowledged that there is such a thing as "rational and moral self-interest" (398). However, King (1998a) warned that there is a potential danger that comes along with humanity's pursuit of the length of life; namely, a situation in which individuals solely pursue their own well-being and "try to live as if nobody else lives in the world but themselves" (126). He feared that when wholly self-indulgent individuals do engage others it is only in order to use them "as mere tools to get to where they're going" (126). In his speech "The Ethical Demands for Integration" King (1986) explained how white Americans' pursuit of the length of life, as manifest in the system of segregation, affected the way in which they conceptualized black humanity: "The tragedy of segregation is that it treats men as means rather than ends, and thereby reduces them to things rather than persons" (119). Consequently, the "traditional southerner is fond of 'his Negro' as he is of a pet or a finely-tooled fire arm. 'It' serves a purpose or gets a job done" (119).

In King's 1960 version of the "Dimensions" sermon he attributed the bulk of America's racial problems to white Americans' dangerous pursuit of the length of life. He stated, "And my friends, I am convinced that this is the basis of our problem in the area of race relations today. This is our problem in the South, and this is our problem over the United States. Many of our white brothers are concerned only about the length of life, their preferred economic positions, their political power, their so-called way of life" (King 2007, 400). Given the grave danger of solely pursuing the length of life, King argued that it must be complemented by the breadth of life. The breadth of life is King's conception of serving others. He postulated that one has not truly begun to live until he or she has moved beyond the myopic concern for oneself and developed a genuine concern for the well-being of others. King seemed to suggest that serving others would provide a check to the excessive individualism that is inculcated in one's pursuit of the "length of life." Accordingly, in his 1954 homily, King (2007) advised the congregation at Dexter Avenue Baptist Church to develop an other-regarding disposition by learning to pray daily in the following manner: "'Lord teach me to unselfishly serve humanity'" (154).

However, as King began to speak out against whites' collective pursuit of the length of life at the expense of blacks in his 1960 sermon, he had to find a means to get members of both races to develop an ethos that was conducive to creating a more just society. Toward this end, King (2007) encouraged Americans to embrace an ethos that promoted political service, which he called "dangerous altruism" (400). King conveyed his conception of dangerous altruism in his "Dimensions" sermons by drawing on one of Jesus's parables, that of the good Samaritan. In the good Samaritan parable Jesus tells of a man who is left for dead by a gang of robbers on the side of the very dangerous Jericho road. Despite the man being on the precipice of death, a priest and a Levite passed him by pretending not to notice his grave condition. However, the third passerby—a Samaritan—not only showed concern by stopping but he also administered aid and ensured that the man's condition was significantly improved. King speculated that perhaps the others did not stop out of sheer fear. According to King, the fear caused those who passed him by to ask, "If I stop to help this man, what will happen to me?" The difference between them and the "good Samaritan" was that the Samaritan reversed the question and asked, "If I do not stop to help this man, what will happen to him?" (400). The importance of the good Samaritan parable is that King used it, just as he did in his "The Drum Major Instinct" sermon, to redefine greatness in terms of one's service to humanity. King said, "Therefore, he was a great man because he had the mental equipment for a dangerous altruism. He was a great man because he could rise above his self-concern to the broader concern of his brother" (400).

In *Where Do We Go from Here* King once again draws on the good Samaritan parable, but this time he uses it to explain what he means by a "revolution of values." King (1968b) offered, "A true revolution of values will soon cause us to question the fairness and justice of many of our past and present policies. We are called to play the Good Samaritan on life's road side, but that will only be an initial act. One day the whole Jericho Road must be transformed so that men and women will not be beaten and robbed as they make their journey through life. True compassion is more than flinging a coin to a beggar, it understands that an edifice which produces beggars, needs restructuring" (198). In King's reinterpretation of the parable the Jericho road has become an analogy for contemporary manifestations of structural injustice. As Iris Marion Young (2011) explains, "Structural injustice, then, exists when social processes put large groups of persons under systematic threat of domination or deprivation of the means to develop and exercise their capacities"; she continues, "at the same time these processes enable others to dominate or to have a wide range of opportunities for developing and exercising capacities available to them" (52). Thus, the Jericho road is meant to represent those social processes that all members of society participate in, which enable some members of society to flourish while simultaneously making others—mostly nonwhite and poor—more vulnerable to domination and deprivation. With this in mind, the endangered man symbolizes those who suffer as a result of structural inequality. As King (2010) explained, the wounded man represents "any needy man—on one of the numerous Jericho roads of life" (22).

To understand how King conceived of structural injustice, it will be helpful to consider two passages from his early "Dimensions" sermons. In King's 1954 "Dimensions" sermon he argued that global capitalism and international commerce have structured the world in such a way that the typical American participates in social processes that impact people all across the world before they even leave the house each morning:

> You get up in the morning and go to the bathroom, and you reach over for a bar of soap, and that's handed to you by a Frenchman. You reach

over for a sponge, and that's given to you by a Turk. You reach over for a towel, and that comes to your hand from the hands of a Pacific Islander. And then you go on to the kitchen to get your breakfast. You reach on over to get a little coffee, and that's poured in your cup by a South American. Or maybe you decide that you want a little tea this morning, only to discover that that's poured in your cup by a Chinese. Or maybe you want a little cocoa, that's poured in your cup by a West African. Then you want a little bread and you reach over to get it, and that's given to you by the hands of an English-speaking farmer, not to mention the baker. Before you get through eating breakfast in the morning, you're dependent on more than half the world. (King 2007, 155)

King introduced this anecdote as a means to make the claim that "all life is involved in a single process so that whatever effects one directly affects all indirectly" (155). By advancing the premise that all of humanity is involved in a single process, King was laying the groundwork for the ensuing claim that we are all responsible for combating the forms of structural injustice that are produced by our being tied into this process.

King reinforced this point in the 1960 version of his "Dimensions" sermon by recounting his recent trip to India. King recalled how he had become depressed as he witnessed such deep poverty during his travels throughout the country. Rather than chalking up the poverty to lack of individual effort on behalf of the Indian people or to a corrupt Indian government, he placed responsibility for their plight on Americans. Reflecting on the poverty, King told his parishioners that he asked himself whether Americans had a responsibility to alleviate the woes of the Indian people. He concluded that they did "because the destiny of the United States is tied up with the destiny of India" (King 2007, 401). At first this sounds like an argument guided by a notion of self-interest properly understood. Instead, King continued, "we should use our vast resources of wealth to aid these undeveloped countries that are undeveloped *because* the people have been dominated politically, exploited economically, segregated, and humiliated across the centuries by foreign powers" (401; emphasis added). We can now see that King's use of "destiny" in reference to the United States and India was not an abstract reference to some point in the future. Rather, King suggests that India's current and past pursuit of its destiny was, and is, inextricably bound to America's imperialist pursuit of its own destiny. Thus, King concluded that Americans are obligated to serve Indians by working to alleviate their poverty because it resulted from American participation in social processes that have dominated and deprived them.[1]

Returning to the good Samaritan parable, we can now see that the Samaritan, who also participates in these social processes, epitomizes King's thoughts about the requirements of service in action. Despite the danger and inconvenience of stopping to help others burdened by structures of injustice, the Samaritan exhibits the love necessary to care about the plight of others. However, if the Samaritan's actions are supposed to be instructive, then they seemingly convey the message that service is merely a supererogatory act of kindness. That is, helping others is a good—but not an obligatory—action. This is why, in his later sermons, speeches, and writings, King made the stronger claim that a true revolution of values requires more than an act of kindness, it also requires a commitment to transforming the edifice that relegates people to life's roadside. This commitment to transform self, others, and structures of injustice is what I have termed King's theory of political service.

From the parable, the following components of King's theory of political service can be distilled: It requires Americans to recognize that society is structured such that all members are caught up in what King (2007) calls "a single process so that whatever effects one directly affects all indirectly" (155). According to King (1965), human interdependence means, "I can never be what I ought to be until you are what you ought to be. And you can never be what you ought to be until I am what I ought to be—this is the interrelated structure of reality." In other words, he argued that no member of society can fully flourish if there are structural barriers that unjustly benefit some while burdening others. The structural interrelatedness of all members of society provides the basis of King's oft-repeated claim that "injustice anywhere is a threat to justice everywhere" (King 1986, 290).

Recognizing the ability of structural injustice to deprive some members of society of the ability to fully flourish, King's theory of political service also requires that Americans cultivate a sense of love and concern for their fellow members of society, which will motivate them to work collectively toward transforming others and structures of injustice. For King, the fact that a Samaritan was the only one to stop and serve the man in need is significant. In King's sermon "On Being a Good Neighbor" (2010) he explained, "The Priest and the Levite saw only a bleeding body, not a human being like themselves. But the good Samaritan will always remind us to remove the cataracts of provincialism from our spiritual eyes and see men as men." He continued, "If the Samaritan had considered the wounded man as a Jew first, he would not have stopped, for the Jews and the Samaritans had no dealings" (24–25). In other words, the Samaritan transformed himself by cultivating a sense of love and care for others—even if that other potentially could have harmed him. As a result of the Samaritan's transformation, he transformed the condition of the wounded man. However, King radicalizes service by arguing that transformation of self and others is incomplete without transforming those structures that create conditions of need in the first place. Therefore, King's theory of political service requires more than merely providing aid to those in need; it requires that members of society become active participants in transforming structures of injustice.

King's theory of political service has one more component that is not explicit in the good Samaritan parable. It is that marginalized peoples' struggles against injustice are considered an essential aspect of service.[2] King's contention is that all members of society have the responsibility to participate in collective forms of resistance, which means that even the oppressed are obligated to engage in political service. In King's 1960 "Dimensions" sermon he offered, "I don't want to give the impression that those individuals who are working to remove the system and those individuals who have been on the oppressed end of the old order must not themselves be concerned about breadth. But I realize that so often in history when oppressed people rise up against their oppression they are too concerned about length too often. It is my firm conviction those of us who have been on the oppressed end of the old order have as much responsibility to be concerned about breadth as anybody else" (King 2005, 575). For King, the black American struggle to secure

a better outcome for their community does not, in and of itself, consti-
tute political service. Thus, he proclaimed, "Our aim must not be merely
to achieve rights for Negroes or rights for colored people." Instead, King
argued, "The aim must never be to do that but to achieve democracy for
everybody" (575–76).

In a 1968 address to the SCLC King provided an illustrative example that ties together the three components of the type of political service he has in mind. In King's speech, he highlights the gallant efforts
of young black Americans, who were not only seeking justice for themselves but who were also enlarging the whole society. According to King,
the youths embraced the revolutionary spirit by resisting American values and structures that contributed to their oppression. In the process
they transformed their white peers into allies who joined them in the
battle to transform structures of injustice. King observed, "When [the
Negro youths] took their struggle to the streets, a new spirit of resistance
was born." White youths, inspired by black Americans and recognizing
their interrelated fates, "stirred into action," and they "formed an alliance that aroused the conscience of the nation." King went on to explain
that the black youths "took non-violent resistance, first employed in
Montgomery, Alabama, in mass dimensions and developed original ap-
plications—sit-ins, freedom rides and wade-ins." They were successful,
King claimed, because "they first transformed themselves. Young Negroes had traditionally imitated whites in dress, conduct and thought in
a rigid middle-class pattern. Now they ceased imitating and began initiating." Rather than privileged whites aiding downtrodden black Americans, King (1968a) said, "Leadership passed into the hands of Negroes,
and their white allies began learning from them" (9). King described
the efforts of black youths and their impact on white Americans as "a
revolutionary and wholesome development for both." King considered
these actions revolutionary because the black youth, by first transforming themselves, transformed their white peers, and together they transformed some of America's most vicious social and political structures of
injustice. Ultimately, the black youth, by collectively struggling to make
America a more just and democratic society for all, provided a service to
the entire nation.

III

Although King lauded the efforts of the youth movement, it is not entirely clear that some of the more radical black youths would have
agreed with his account of their actions. In fact, King (1968a) even acknowledged that the greatest contribution of the radical black youths
was their call for "action—direct, self-transforming and structure-
transforming action." What is conspicuously missing from their call to
action is King's emphasis on other-transforming action. In fact, King's
emphasis on transforming white Americans put him at odds with many
youths who espoused the Black Power ideology. In at least one strand of
Black Power, whites were viewed as being devoid of a conscience, and
therefore there was an outright rejection of the need to be preoccupied
with their transformation. In *Where Do We Go from Here* (1968b) King
explained: "Some Black Power advocates consider an appeal to conscience irrelevant" (61). Replying to one such advocate who told King:
"'To hell with conscience and morality. We want power,'" he offered,
"But power and morality must go together, implementing, fulfilling and
ennobling each other." King said, "Nonviolence is power, but it is the
right and good use of power. Constructively it can save the white man as
well as the Negro" (61).

In part due to his concern with transforming white Americans, King
was an unwavering proponent of nonviolent direct action. Nonviolent
direct action, for King, meant that individuals should take up the cause
for justice by way of a peaceful collective process. According to King, the
morality of nonviolence is that it does not "substitute one evil for another" in the same way that violent retaliation does. Ultimately, King
believed that engaging in violence not only inflicts pain on others but
it also damages one's own soul. As King (1968b) explained, "I am concerned that Negroes achieve full status as citizens and as human beings
here in the United States. But I am also concerned about our moral up-
rightness and the health of our souls" (66).

For King, nonviolent direct action is not a passive form of protest. Instead, he insisted that the goal of nonviolent direct action is to create a
scenario that causes a confrontation aimed at dramatizing and elimi-

nating the suffering of the least well off in society. As King (1968b) explained, "Freedom is not won by a passive acceptance of suffering.
Freedom is won by a struggle *against* suffering" (20; emphasis original).
Given King's firm belief that white Americans possess a conscience, he
argued that by suffering in the struggle for justice, black Americans can
redeem the soul of the nation. In order to fully understand King's position, one must recall the central role of God in his conception of humanity. For King, the redemptive quality of suffering is derived from the
Christian love ethic of *agape*. King (2010) defined *agape* as "understanding and creative, redemptive goodwill for all men" (46). Rooted in love
for all of God's creations, King insisted that blacks extend redemptive
goodwill to whites since "*agape* is the love of God operating in the human heart . . . we love every man because God loves him" (46).

King's insistence on *agape* is important since he always distinguished
between three types of love: *eros, philia*, and *agape*. King described
both *eros* and *philia* as being derived from some form of sentimentality. *Eros* is love that is predicated on a strong desire for an object or a
person, while *philia* is derived from some likeable quality that the other
person possesses. According to King (2010), it is this absence of sentimentality that distinguishes *agape* from the other types of love, since it
is the only "love that seeks nothing in return" (45). King argues that a
love that seeks nothing in return is necessary in the struggle for justice
because black Americans cannot depend on a reciprocal sentimentality
from white Americans. Furthermore, white American intransigence led
King to conclude that black Americans cannot rely on "ethical appeals
and persuasion" without some form of "constructive coercive power" in
their quest for justice. As a result, King (1968b) proclaims, "every ethical appeal to the conscience of the white man must be accomplished by
nonviolent pressure" (137).

Beyond the moral argument, King holds that unless black Americans
embraced nonviolence it would not be practical for America to ever become a truly integrated society. While violence may be effective in certain colonial struggles where the ultimate goal is the vanquishing of an
oppressor, King believed that the American context is different since it
exists within a multiracial society. To King (1968b), the interdependence

of the races means that "liberation cannot come without integration and integration cannot come without liberation" (64). He proclaimed, "In the struggle for national independence one can talk about liberation now and integration later, but in the struggle for racial justice in a multiracial society where the oppressor and the oppressed are both 'at home,' liberation must come through integration" (64).

Although King long championed racial integration, his views on the subject evolved considerably over time. Take, for instance, King's discussion of the differences between the concepts of desegregation and integration from the early 1960s. King (1986) observed that although "desegregation and integration are often used interchangeably, there is a great deal of difference between the two. In the context of what our national community needs, desegregation alone is empty and shallow. We must always be aware of the fact that our ultimate goal is integration, and that desegregation is only a first step on the road to the good society" (118). King defined integration in contrast to desegregation, which he said is a negative concept that merely seeks to eliminate the "legal and social prohibitions" that have become systematized in the form of segregation. "Integration," though, "is the positive acceptance of desegregation and the welcomed participation of Negroes into the total range of human activities. Integration is genuine intergroup, interpersonal living" (118). In other words, early on King understood that in the quest for justice, desegregation is necessary but not sufficient. But notice how King also stressed both whites' "acceptance" and their welcoming of the participation of black Americans. As noted, advocates of Black Power largely eschewed this preoccupation with whites as a form of assimilation.

By the late 1960s one can clearly see the profound impact that the ideology of Black Power was beginning to have on King's political thought. The influence of Black Power will come into sharper focus if we consider the challenge to integration leveled by perhaps the most prominent spokesmen of one strand of the Black Power movement—Kwame Ture (Stokely Carmichael) and Charles V. Hamilton. These two thinkers dismissed integrating with whites as a means to real power accumulation by black Americans for two reasons. First, they believed that, instead of seeking power for all black Americans, integration was a ploy for a few successful blacks to be able to live in white neighborhoods. According to Ture and Hamilton, the kind of integration that is championed by the black middle class "has meant that a few blacks 'make it,' leaving the black community behind, sapping it of leadership potential and know-how" (Carmichael and Hamilton 1967, 53). They argued that black Americans needed to obtain real political, economic, and psychological power as a unit if they were to truly become self-determining human beings. However, they felt that the type of integration that was advanced by privileged black Americans benefitted them as individuals but had little or no positive effect on black Americans as a collective unit.

Ture and Hamilton's second concern with the goal of integration was that, rather than serving as a means of sharing power with black Americans, they viewed integration as a way for white Americans to maintain a firm grip on power. Additionally, they charged that black Americans' goal of moving into white neighborhoods only served to undermine blacks' attempts to equalize their social standing with white Americans. They assert, "[Integration] is based on complete acceptance of the fact that in order to have a decent house or education, black people must move into a white neighborhood or send their children to a white school." They continue, "This reinforces, among both black and white, the idea that 'white' is automatically superior and 'black' is by definition inferior. For this reason, 'integration' is a subterfuge for the maintenance of white supremacy" (Carmichael and Hamilton 1967, 54). In sum, Ture and Hamilton maintained that integration would only benefit a few privileged blacks and it would do nothing to disrupt the stranglehold of power that whites enjoyed over blacks or challenge white norms.

If Ture and Hamilton are correct, then the effects of integration on the black community are potentially the same, if not worse, than those derived from segregation. In both instances, black Americans are firmly subordinated in relation to white Americans. However, one can make the case that Ture and Hamilton are able to reach this conclusion because they are not, in fact, accurately describing integration; instead, what they are describing is assimilation. Assimilation is the idea that in order to achieve any semblance of equality, black Americans must wholly adopt white American values and culture. The paradox, as Ture and Hamilton correctly point out, is that as blacks adopt white values and culture in an attempt to gain social standing they are, in turn, furthering their own subordination. For this reason, Ture and Hamilton believed that the avenue to black empowerment was for black Americans to gain control over their own communities, thereby integrating with white Americans on more equitable terms—if at all.

In part because of the challenge leveled by Ture and Hamilton, King, over time, began to change his tenor when discussing integration.[3] In 1967 King retained his belief that integration is "true intergroup, interpersonal living." However, he added that integration required "the mutual sharing of power" (King 1968b, 64). In this sense, King was building on his earlier conception of integration. King said, "I cannot see how the Negro will be totally liberated from the crushing weight of poor education, squalid housing and economic strangulation until he is integrated, with power, into every level of American life" (64). It is important to underscore that King is defining true integration as a complete structural transformation of American society; one in which black Americans are politically, socially, and economically empowered. Realizing that white acceptance and their embracement of the welcomed participation of black Americans was problematic, King (1986) critiqued his earlier notion of integration: "I think in the past all too often we did it that way. We talked of integration in romantic and esthetic terms and it ended up as merely adding color to a still predominately white power structure" (666). What King gradually came to understand was that integration, as it was implemented in the 1960s, denuded blacks of power. As an example, King cited those blacks who held positions of power within all-black organizations—such as teachers associations—but were forced to give up their power once they integrated into all-white organizations. In response, King demanded, "We don't want to be integrated out of power; we want to be integrated into power" (666).

As we can see, King fully agreed with Ture and Hamilton about the need for blacks to accumulate power. According to King (1968b), "Power, properly understood, is the ability to achieve purpose. It is the strength required to bring about social, political or economic changes" (37). However, Ture and Hamilton believed that blacks needed to build up separate bases of power prior to any consideration of integration. Since they were beginning with the premise that black Americans were colonized by white America, their overall goal was to break the relationship of blacks' dependence on whites. Therefore, Ture and Hamilton understood the goal of Black Power as the need to "correct the approach to dependency, to remove that dependency, and to establish a viable psychological, political and social base on which the black community can function to meet its needs" (Carmichael and Hamilton 1967, 81). They believed that blacks could eventually enter into alliances with whites, but they did not view this as a primary concern. As they succinctly put it, "Black Power simply says: enter coalitions only after you are able to 'stand on your own'" (81). King, on the other hand, was convinced that black Americans could not accumulate enough power to transform structures of injustice without help from other races. He concluded, "In short, the Negroes' problem cannot be solved unless the whole of American society takes a new turn toward greater economic justice" (King 1968b, 51). In essence, the source of disagreement among King and the advocates of Black Power was not on the issue of coalition building, per se, but about what it would take to get American society to make that turn toward economic justice.

Ture and Hamilton believe that the greater American society will embrace economic justice for black people once blacks, themselves, possess enough power to force the issue. They explain, "The concept of Black Power rests on a fundamental premise: *Before a group can enter the open society, it must first close ranks.* By this we mean that group solidarity is necessary before a group can operate effectively from a bargaining position of strength in a pluralistic society" (Carmichael and Hamilton 1967, 44; emphasis original). They go on to cite the various ethnic groups who immigrated to America as examples of their approach, a point that King vociferously disputed. He retorted that these groups did not, in fact, rise to power through separatism. They did so, he contended, by forming alliances with other groups. King (1968b) declared, "To succeed in a pluralistic society, and an often hostile one at that, the Negro obviously needs organized strength, but that strength will only be effective when it is consolidated through constructive alliances" (51). Yet, as King grew increasingly frustrated with whites' unwillingness to confront their own racism,[4] he once again gravitated toward a position strikingly similar to that of Ture and Hamilton. To be clear, King always remained firmly committed to integration as an end goal; however, in the late 1960s he reluctantly admitted that "there are some situations where separation may serve as a temporary way-station" (King 1986, 666–67). King's embracement of a separatist position raises the obvious question of whether or not transforming the other remained a key component in his theory of political service.

IV

In order to gain a greater sense of how separation fit into King's theory of service, it is helpful to consider a concrete example of what King had in mind when he endorsed separation as a temporary way station to integration. In 1966 King decided to move with his family to Chicago's Lawndale neighborhood. The purpose of King's move was to join with local Chicagoans in an effort to transform those structures of injustice that forced black Americans to languish in impoverished ghettos (Ralph 1993). Unfortunately, these efforts were largely stymied by white opposition and the shrewd maneuverings of Chicago's mayor, Richard Daley (Fairclough 1987; Branch 1998; Garrow 2004). Despite these setbacks, King continued to push for complete integration of housing in American cities. However, he also realized that the failure of whites to own up to their own racism meant that blacks would need to concentrate on building up the ghettos as they worked toward creating a more integrated American society.

To understand King's delicate position, consider that he vehemently denounced what he viewed as the dual housing market—one black, one

white—in every city, which would seem to be remedied by calling for
the complete and immediate integration of each city. Yet, as a solution,
he proposed,

> In every city, to deal with this unjust dualism, we must constantly work
> toward the goal of a truly integrated society while at the same time we
> enrich the ghetto. We must seek to enrich the ghetto immediately in the
> sense of improving the housing conditions, improving the schools in the
> ghetto, improving the economic conditions. At the same time, we must
> be working to open the housing market so there will be one housing
> market only. We must work on two levels. We should gradually move to
> disperse the ghetto, and immediately move to improve conditions within
> the ghetto, which in the final analysis will make it possible to disperse it
> at a greater rate a few years from now. (King 1986, 667)

Here, King made what he believes is a pragmatic argument that embraces a temporary form of segregation while blacks seek to equalize their psychological and material resources with whites living in all-
white neighborhoods.[5] Like Ture and Hamilton, King called for a form
of separatism that can serve as a "bargaining position to get to that ultimate goal, which is a truly integrated society where there is shared
power" (666). However, unlike Ture and Hamilton, King also suggested
that while blacks were building up their resources in the ghettos there
should be a gradual dispersal of blacks into white communities. The desegregation of white communities was meant to increase the exposure
of black and white Americans to one another. King believed that the in-
creased exposure of the races would heighten the possibility that alliances could be formed. King did not deny that the gradual dispersal of
black Americans into white communities would be a painful and difficult experience for both races. Nonetheless, King (1968b) explained,
"Like life, racial understanding is not something that we find but something we must create" (28). American race relations, King argued, can
only improve if individuals are able to interact in nonsegregated living
spaces, which create opportunities for transformation to take place.
"Desegregation will not change attitudes but it will provide the contact

and confrontation necessary by which integration is made possible and attainable" (123).[6]

Whereas Ture and Hamilton objected to alliances with white Americans until black Americans had a firmly established power base, King argued that alliances with white Americans are essential to achieving structural change—in housing or otherwise. According to King (1968b), "The larger economic problems confronting the Negro community will only be solved by federal programs involving billions of dollars," which will require an "alliance of liberal-labor-civil-rights forces" (51). Consistent with King's theory of political service, he rejected the view that "the maximum use of legislation, welfare and antipoverty programs has now replaced demonstrations, and that overt and visible protest should now be abandoned" (139). Rather than letting up, King argued that blacks must first transform themselves by developing a "rugged sense of somebodyness" and "group identity" (130). Next, they must exhibit a sense of *agape* in their commitment to transforming their white peers and structures of injustice by engaging in mass nonviolent demonstrations. However, King argued that mass demonstrations are not enough and that they needed to be supplemented by "the task of organizing people into permanent groups to protect their own interests and produce change in their own behalf" (139). Finally, white Americans also needed to recognize that they are inextricably bound with black Americans and thus need to exhibit their own form of *agape* by continuing to support the civil rights movement.

Even if the number of white Americans who are initially committed to such a cause is small, King (1968b) proclaimed, "That creative minority of Whites absolutely committed to civil rights can make it clear to the larger society that vacillation and procrastination on the question of racial justice can no longer be tolerated" (101). Underscoring the transformative impact of political service on the greater society, King declared, "It will take such a small committed minority to work unrelentingly to win the uncommitted majority. Such a group may well transform America's greatest dilemma into her most glorious opportunity" (101).

As a means of crystallizing how King's theory of political service re-
mains relevant for our contemporary struggles against structural injustice, it may be helpful to quote his critique of Black Power at length: "In
the final analysis the weakness of Black Power is its failure to see that
the black man needs the white man and the white man needs the black
man. However much we may try to romanticize the slogan, there is no
separate black path to power and fulfillment that does not intersect
white paths, and there is no separate white path to power and fulfillment, short of social disaster, that does not share that power with black
aspirations for freedom and human dignity" (King 1968b, 54). Not only
does this passage underscore King's unyielding commitment to integration but it also brings us full circle to his "The Drum Major Instinct" and
"Dimensions" sermons. Although King is critiquing a position that he
attributes to advocates of Black Power, he is really rejecting a broader
worldview that configures human beings as individuals whose sole pursuit of the length of one's life comes at the expense of others. Instead,
King is positing a configuration of humanity that recognizes that humans can only fully flourish when the length of life is complemented by
the breadth of life. Therefore, King is calling on all of us to redefine greatness in terms of our political service to others. This is a lesson that seems
more relevant than ever in our contemporary neoliberal moment.

CHAPTER 2
THE AMERICAN DREAM

America is essentially a dream, a dream yet unfulfilled. The substance of the dream is expressed in some very familiar words found in the Declaration of Independence. "We hold these truths to be self-evident: that all men are created equal; that they are endowed by their Creator with certain inalienable rights; that among these are life, liberty, and the pursuit of happiness." This is a dream.
—MARTIN LUTHER KING JR.

I

On August 28, 2013, President Barack Obama delivered a stirring speech at a national ceremony commemorating the fiftieth anniversary of the March on Washington for Jobs and Freedom. In his address, Obama paid homage to the many participants in the civil rights movement, including Martin Luther King Jr., whose efforts helped to change the course of American history. Obama observed that, in addition to securing legal protections, the civil rights movement sought to improve the economic lot for all Americans. After articulating King's call for the United States to provide black Americans with the basic resources necessary to reach their fullest potential as members of American society, Obama folded King's position into the language of the American dream. He said, "What King was describing has been the dream of every American. It's what's lured for centuries new arrivals to our shores" (Obama 2013). Acknowledging the unfinished business of the civil rights movement, Obama declared that much more work is necessary to make the American dream a possibility for all. "And it's along this second dimension—of economic opportunity, the chance through honest toil to advance one's station in life—where the goals of 50 years ago have fallen most short" (Obama 2013). According to Obama, King and the many

other participants in the civil rights movement not only serve as shin-
ing examples of courage and determination but also represent a dream
yet unfulfilled.

Obama's decision to frame King's political and economic commitments in the language of the American dream demonstrates what scholars refer to as the deradicalization of King's legacy (Harding 1996; Dyson
2000; Singh 2004; West 2015; Glaude 2016). This is because within contemporary parlance the American dream has come to mean that with
enough hard work anyone can achieve upward mobility in either economic or social terms (Hochschild 1995; Cullen 2003; Hanson and Zogby
2010). The underlying assumption of this neoliberal ideology is that
America is a fundamentally just nation that guarantees freedom and
equality for all its citizens, regardless of one's initial status. King (1968b),
however, rejects this basic premise and instead contends that achieving
equality for the black and poor will require nothing short of a "radical
restructuring of the architecture of American society" (141). King argues
that structural reform means that, at the very least, Americans must collectively organize to demand a redistribution of wealth that will provide
the resources necessary for a guaranteed annual income to all members
of American society. Ironically, while commemorating King's contribution to the March on Washington, Obama rebuked calls for such a radical redistribution of wealth with a thinly veiled paternalistic critique of
black and poor Americans. He offered, "And what had once been a call
for equality of opportunity, the chance for all Americans to work hard
and get ahead was too often framed as a mere desire for government
support—as if we had no agency in our own liberation, as if poverty was
an excuse for not raising your child, and the bigotry of others was reason
to give up on yourself" (Obama 2013).

By framing King's legacy within the American dream language,
Obama not only undermined King's call for a radical restructuring
of American society but the president also downplayed King's call for
collective, political action aimed at structural reform. At the apex of
Obama's speech he called on his audience to emulate the examples of
everyday Americans who are continuing to march in the spirit of the
civil rights movement. However, Obama only offered examples of indi-

viduals who are engaged in apolitical, supererogatory acts of kindness to others. For example, Obama cited "that tireless teacher who gets to class early and stays late and dips into her own pocket to buy supplies because she believes that every child is her charge—she's marching," or "that successful businessman who doesn't have to but pays his workers a fair wage and then offers a shot to a man, maybe an ex-con who is down on his luck—he's marching" (Obama 2013). After giving a few more examples, Obama (2013) concluded his speech by articulating how contemporary Americans might embody the message bequeathed by those in attendance at the March on Washington: "Everyone who realizes what those glorious patriots knew on that day—that change does not come from Washington, but to Washington; that change has always been built on our willingness, We The People, to take on the mantle of citizenship—you are marching." However, given the examples offered by Obama it is not entirely clear how these individual acts of kindness translate into the type of massive collective action advocated by King and demonstrated by the participants in the March on Washington (Dawson and Francis 2016).

Obama's speech illustrates the ways in which King's commitment to a radical form of political service is easily sanitized. This is, in part, due to the fact that King often invoked the American dream when articulating his vision of a future American society. As Eric Sundquist (2009) points out, "By the time there was a national holiday in King's honor, his dream had become virtually equivalent to the American dream" (26). Despite the connection between King's dream and the American dream in the American public imagination, Cornel West (2015) reminds us, "King indeed had a dream. But it was not the American dream" (xi). If West is right, then King's repeated use of the term "American dream" when articulating his own dream raises a series of questions. What was King's conception of the American dream? What actions did King believe were required to bring the American dream to fruition? Who was King's target audience when he invoked the language of the American dream? One argument about King's use of the American dream is that he strategically invoked this language as an idiom to call on white Americans to uphold the American creed (Cone 1991).[1] While I do not completely disagree with this claim, in this chapter I focus on King's invocation of the American dream while addressing black audiences. More specifically, I argue that King's understanding and use of the American dream cannot be divorced from his theory of political service. In other words, for King the American dream represented a more inclusive America in which the universal principles of liberty, equality, and respect for the dignity and worth of all human beings *could only come about when Americans, but especially black Americans, engaged in self-transforming and other-transforming collective action aimed at combating structural injustice.*

In what follows, I explore King's conception and use of the American dream. I do so by analyzing a range of King's speeches and written texts in which he invokes the American dream, but I pay special attention to a series of his speeches entitled "The American Dream." These speeches are an ideal unit of analysis because they provide King's clearest articulation of his understanding of the American dream. Furthermore, he delivers these speeches over a wide swath of his public career, thereby providing an opportunity to be attentive to the ways in which his conception of the American dream evolved over time. My analysis of King's speeches reveals that embedded within them are what I have identified as the three components of political service. For instance, in his "The American Dream" speeches, King (2007) implores Americans to recognize that society is structured such that all of its members are "involved in a single process so that whatever effects one directly affects all indirectly" (155). King argues that humanity's interdependence is derived from his belief that God created all of humanity. Thus, all Americans are human beings worthy of equal dignity and respect. Once established, he then implores Americans to cultivate a sense of love and concern for their fellow members of society, which will motivate them to work collectively toward transforming themselves and others but also structures of injustice. Finally, King uses the American dream to emphasize black Americans' obligation to exercise their political agency by taking up their own cause for justice. The fact that King embedded these three components within all of his most explicit discussions of the American dream underscores my claim that King's conception and use of the American dream cannot be divorced from his theory of political service.

Revisiting King's conception and use of the American dream can be extremely helpful for contemporary Americans seeking to galvanize marginalized populations to struggle toward creating structural change within our contemporary neoliberal moment. The fact that the American dream enjoys wide appeal among Americans means, when integrated with King's theory of political service, it can still be a useful political tool. It is my hope that my argument will not only challenge attempts to divorce King's legacy from structural change and collective action but also restore the radical possibilities of the American dream as a political concept.

II

Before specifically engaging King's conception and use of the American dream, I must first address an obvious question: why should anyone who is seeking to create a more just and democratic society concern themselves with the strategic invocation of the American dream? The answer is quite simple: whether we like it or not, the American dream has become an ideology that blankets our everyday lives. It influences our society's priorities, it affects the way we interact with our neighbors, it informs how we structure our schools and corporations, and it is reflected in policy choices by lawmakers. In fact, the idea of the American dream is so pervasive that when Jim Cullen (2003) began conducting research for his book about the subject he found that its definition is "virtually taken for granted. It's as if no one feels compelled to fix the meanings and uses of a term everyone presumably understands—which today appears to mean that in the United States anything is possible if you want it badly enough" (12). Citing the fact that media, athletes, politicians, and even businessmen all invoke the American dream in their varied endeavors, Cullen concludes, "The term seems like the most lofty as well as the most immediate component of an American identity, a birthright far more meaningful and compelling than terms like 'democracy,' 'Constitution,' or even 'the United States'" (12). In other words, the American dream has become shorthand for what it means to be American and thus has currency that can possibly be leveraged for positive purposes.

As Cullen notes, despite the prevalence of the American dream ideology there is no fixed definition among the public or even within the scholarly literature (Hochschild 1995; Cullen 2003; Hanson and Zogby 2010). "Nevertheless," political scientist Jennifer Hochschild (1995) observes, "the phrase elicits for most Americans some variant of [John] Locke's fantasy—a new world where anything can happen and good things might" (15). In other words, the American dream posits that America is an exceptional place where economic and social success is obtainable by anyone, as long as an individual is willing to work hard enough to achieve it. In contemporary American society, the American dream is largely interpreted within a neoliberal and color-blind framework. For many it has come to mean that with the abolition of legal racial discrimination, America is a fundamentally just nation that provides freedom and equality of opportunity for all members of society, regardless of one's station in life. Consequently, the American dream as an ideology implies that the fate of an individual's life outcome is owing almost exclusively to one's work ethic, and it does not take into consideration the way in which structural inequality may impact life outcomes.

King, however, rejected any interpretation of the American dream that did not grapple with the devastating effects of structural inequality on the lives of the least well off in society. King's conception of the American dream, according to James Cone (1991), was a combination of the "liberal democratic tradition, as defined by the Declaration of Independence and the Constitution, and the biblical tradition of the Old and New Testaments, as interpreted by Protestant liberalism and the black church" (66). Drawing from these two traditions, King conceived of the American dream as a universal promise of liberty, equality, and the recognition of the dignity and worth of all of humanity. To King, though, the American dream was not to be understood as something that would be self-fulfilling. Instead, King believed that all Americans were required to engage in a form of political service aimed at restructuring American society so that the nation could finally make good on its promises to all its members.

The underlying premise of King's conception of the American dream is that America, despite being plagued by racism, is redeemable. In King's final book, *Where Do We Go from Here*, he compares America to a character in one of Jesus's parables—the prodigal son. In this parable Jesus tells a story of a young man who came of age and decided to leave his father's house in search of adventure, but the farther he moved away from the house the more he met with despair. The young man eventually ran out of money, and once, during a famine, he became so desperate for food that he sought a meal in a pig's trough. One day the young man suddenly came to his senses and realized that he must return to his home. According to King (1968b), America is the prodigal son who drifted to the "far country of racism" and who left behind a home that was "solidly structured idealistically" (88–89).

It is important to notice that the structure of this home was provided by the very same values that compose King's conception of the American dream. King (1968b) explained that its pillars were: "All men are made in the image of God; all men are brothers; all men are created equal; every man is heir to a legacy of dignity and worth; every man has rights that are neither conferred by nor derived from the state, they are God-given." King continued by affirming that it is not too late to take action in order to make democracy a reality for all. "If America would come to herself and return to her true home, 'one nation, indivisible, with liberty and justice for all,' she would give the democratic creed a new authentic ring, enkindle the imagination of mankind and fire the souls of men" (89). King's use of such terms as "fundamental" and "return" in the quoted passages seem to indicate that he wanted America to revert to a moment in history when the nation did not embrace a racist ideology. However, as I explain below, when King urged for a return to something more fundamental, he is not urging for a return to some utopian past; rather, he is calling on America to make good on the promises that were espoused at the time of the nation's founding.

King's call for a commitment to the nation's purportedly fundamental principles seemingly echoes a problematic argument made by the Swedish sociologist Gunnar Myrdal. Myrdal (1944) claimed that despite the fact that many of America's practices were in direct contradiction to its professed creed of equality, these contradictory practices would eventually become aligned with its principle of equality. Myrdal's argument was rooted in a deeply held belief that any human could change if only he or she was presented with facts. Political theorist Joel Olson, for one, is deeply skeptical of this distinction. Olson's concern is that Myrdal's dichotomy between the American creed and its practices works to insulate American democratic ideals from the taint of racism. Rather than viewing such American atrocities as slavery and Jim Crow legislation as unfortunate blips that violated the egalitarian ethos of American democracy, Olson suggests that we understand these episodes as both in violation of democratic ideals and also constitutive of them. For Olson (2004), "Racial oppression makes full democracy impossible, but it has also made American democracy possible. Conversely, American democracy has made racial oppression possible, for neither slavery nor segregation nor any other form of racial domination could have survived without the tacit or explicit consent of the white majority" (xv). Ultimately, Olson concludes, "American democracy is a white democracy, a polity ruled in the interests of a white citizenry and characterized by simultaneous relations of equality and privilege: equality among whites, who are privileged in relation to those who are not white" (xv). However, the problem with Myrdal's creeds/practices distinction is that it places American democracy beyond reproach and consequently leaves its racist foundations unquestioned.

As we can see from Olson's critique, if King's call for a return to a set of universal American principles did indeed unquestioningly embrace Myrdal's creeds/practices distinction, then this is very problematic. However, despite seemingly upholding Myrdal's problematic creeds/practices dichotomy in *Where Do We Go from Here*, King moved beyond Myrdal to offer a more complicated understanding of American history. King (1968b) pointed to America's contradictions by bluntly charging that "white America has had a schizophrenic personality on the question of race. She has been torn between selves—a self in which she proudly professed the great principles of democracy and a self in which she sadly practiced the antithesis of democracy" (72). Although beginning with the Myrdalian framework, King went on to demand, "For the good of America, it is necessary to refute the idea that the dominant ideology in our country even today is freedom and equality while racism is just an occasional departure from the norm on the part of a few bigoted extremists" (73). The power of King's critique comes through when he says of racism and democracy, "Of the two dominant and contradictory strains in the American psyche, the positive one, our democratic heritage, was the later development on the American continent" (74). Here King was not only suggesting that racism has always existed in America but that racism predated American democracy. In other words, King was not susceptible to Olson's critique of Myrdal's creed/practices dichotomy because King was not seeking to insulate democracy from the stain of American racism.

Furthermore, King argued that the institutionalization of slavery prior to the nation's founding had the effect of contradicting and qualifying America's claims to be a democratic society. King (1968b) charged, "Slavery was not only ignored in defining democracy, but its enlargement was tolerated in the interests of strengthening the nation" (75). King claimed that although slavery was initially implemented for the economic enrichment of white Americans, it also "had a profound impact in shaping the social-political-legal structure of the nation. Land and slaves were the chief forms of private property, property was wealth and the voice of wealth made the laws and determined politics" (76). Here King was arguing that white men, by possessing a disproportionate influence over politics, *democratically* reduced black Americans to "propertyless property" and "stripped [them] of all human and civil rights" (76). If, as King claimed, "this degradation was sanctioned and protected by institutions of government," then the inverse is also true; namely, that white Americans' privilege was also sanctioned and protected by those same institutions (76). Even that great document of freedom and equality, the Declaration of Independence, was, to King, a celebration of white privilege. He proclaimed, "Jefferson's majestic words, 'all men are created equal,' meant for him, as for many others, that all *white* men are created equal" (81; emphasis original).

After offering a brief history of American racism, King ultimately concluded that the problem with his white peers is that they have never fully admitted to themselves the depth of racism in American society. King's description of how white Americans evaded American racism is eerily similar to the approach taken by today's color-blind conservatives. King charged that too many of his contemporaries have been deluded into believing that America is a fundamentally just society and that racial inequality is simply the result of an individual's failure to take responsibility for his or her life's outcome. Pushing back against this rationale, King (1968b) declared, "It would be neither true nor honest to say that the Negro's status is what it is because he is innately inferior or because he is basically lazy and listless or because he has not sought to lift himself by his own bootstraps" (71). Rather than attributing racial inequalities in America to the failures of individual black Americans, King suggested, "To find the origins of the Negro problem we must turn to the white man's problem" (71). King claimed that, historically, the problem for white Americans has been "the haunting ambivalence, the intellectual and moral recognition that slavery is wrong, but the emotional tie to the system so deep and pervasive that it imposes an inflexible unwillingness to root it out" (80–81). This ambivalence continues to haunt America since many white Americans profess a commitment to equality for all, while they also maintain an emotional investment in the status quo of race relations (Dovidio and Gaertner 1986; Bonilla-Silva 2003).

King believed that white Americans would have to make a conscious commitment to justice if they were ever going to move beyond this ambivalence. With this in mind, one can see why King (1968b), when quoting Myrdal, italicizes one sentence in particular: "*America is free to choose whether the Negro shall remain her liability or become her opportunity*" (90). However, unlike Myrdal, King did not feel that white Americans would make this conscious choice once they were presented with the facts of their inconsistencies. Instead, he insisted, "The Negro has not gained a single right in America without persistent pressure and agitation. However lamentable it may seem, the Negro is now convinced that white America will never admit to him equal rights unless it is coerced into doing it" (96). Unfortunately, according to King, the America dream could not be divorced from the requirement that black Americans engage in political service by collectively striving to secure the conditions of equality for all Americans.

III

Although King's theory of political service requires all members of society to work toward transforming structures of injustice, it also places a special emphasis on the role of black Americans in restructuring American society. In hindsight, it may seem strange that King would fold the American dream into his theory of political service; especially when appealing to black Americans. Embedded within the American dream ideology is not only the denial of structural inequality but also a glorification of economic and social ascension, both of which were largely denied to black Americans. However, King also understood that the American dream was not just an ideology but that it is also a symbol of what it means to be American. As anthropologist David Kertzer (1988) explains, "[Symbols] are a means, indeed the primary means, by which we give meaning to the world around us; they allow us to interpret what we see, and, indeed, what we are" (4). Although black Americans were excluded from this symbol of Americanism, King knew that this did not always have to be the case. As Kertzer explains, "Though symbols give people a way of understanding the world, it is people who produce new symbols and transform the old" (5). King, as a member of an oppressed segment of the population, understood that "identifying oneself with a popular symbol can be a potent means of gaining and keeping power, for the hallmark of power is the construction of reality" (Kertzer 1988, 5).

In order to effectively identify blacks with the symbol of the American dream, King had to "blacken" those American promises previously held out solely for white Americans. As George Shulman (2008) explains, "A racist culture makes blackness a mark of embodiment that 'stains' the spirit and the political, black entry into the symbolic defeats the abstraction that makes equality 'white' by making rights disembodied" (116). In other words, by blackening the American dream, King was asserting to black audiences that the promises it came to symbolize could no longer be understood as applying exclusively to white Americans. Furthermore, by identifying black Americans with the promises embodied in the American dream, King was providing a seemingly powerless people with the psychological tools necessary to exercise their political power (Allen 2004). Ultimately, my claim is that when King invoked the American dream, he was not seeking to reify its underlying ideology; rather, he was transforming this symbol of white economic and social mobility into a symbol of black political struggle for freedom and equality.

Seeking to blacken the American dream, it makes sense that many of the speeches in which King explicitly invokes the American dream were delivered before predominately black audiences. Examples include both his 1960 "The Negro and the American Dream" (King 2005, 508–11), his 1961 "The American Dream" (King 1986, 206–16) speech, and his 1965 speech by the same title (King 1998a, 79–100). These speeches were delivered to several branches of the South Carolina NAACP, to the graduating class of the historically black Lincoln University, and to King's Ebenezer Baptist Church, respectively. In fact, King even implicitly invokes the tenets of the American dream to call on black Americans to exercise their political power in his first speech as president of the Montgomery Improvement Association. Yet, King made a large shift from his 1955 address before the black American community of Montgomery and his later, more explicit appeals to the American dream in the 1960s. It is worth examining these changes.

As early as King's 1955 speech at Holt Street Baptist Church, he made explicit his beliefs about the need for black Americans to engage in political service by working to eradicate racial inequality. King, in essence, began his involvement in the civil rights movement by making a case for service as a central component of what it means to be an American citizen. This can be seen in his explanation of why it is that the black community of Montgomery decided to come together to protest the bus line. King (2001) said, "We are here in a general sense because first and foremost we are American citizens, and we are determined to apply our citizenship to the fullness of its meaning" (7). For King, active participation in the cause for justice was the means by which democracy became real. He continued, "We are here also because of our love for democracy, because of our deep-seated belief that democracy transformed from thin paper to thick action is the greatest form of government on earth" (7). According to King, a full application of citizenship meant that black Americans must demand justice by exercising their "right to protest for right" (9).

Notice that on this particular night King did not need to convince his Montgomery audience of the need to engage in political service. The daily assaults on the dignity of black Americans by their white peers had reached a boiling point, and many in the black community had already assumed responsibility for seeking justice (Garrow 2004). Accordingly, King's use of the American dream was an effort to sustain the black community's determination to continue their boycott by assuring them that they were justified in their cause. "We are not wrong in what we are doing. If we are wrong, then the Supreme Court of this Nation is wrong. If we are wrong the Constitution of the United States is wrong. If we are wrong God Almighty is wrong" (King 2001, 10).

King's rhetorical strategy of justifying the actions of the boycotters by invoking the Supreme Court and the Constitution was meant to convey that the American dream held out a promise of legally protected rights to all American citizens. The reason this was a source of motivation among Montgomery's black community was that it directly contradicted the way in which they had been relegated to second-class citizenship by their white peers. King's speech sought to affirm black American citizenship and to assert that the decisions handed down by the Supreme Court and the rights articulated in the Constitution applied as equally to them as they did to white Americans. It is important to note that King's conception of justice had not yet developed into a call for complete integration of the black and white races; in fact, early in the Montgomery campaign King was not even calling for the end of segregation (Cone 1991; Marsh 2005). Therefore, King's use of the American dream was subtle and was not employed to make straightforward appeals for power sharing between black and white Americans. The form of justice that King initially called for was simply that black Americans be treated fairly under the law.

As King's involvement in the civil rights movement evolved, so, too, did his demands. Consequently, he actively sought to recruit black Americans into the battle for justice. It is at this point that we see King move away from a subtle invocation of the American dream to a more explicit appeal to the great American symbol. Evidence of this can be seen in King's 1961 commencement address at Lincoln University entitled "The American Dream." King would deliver some variation of this speech several times over the next several years. In these speeches, King provided an explicit argument about Americans' responsibility to engage in political service by remaking America into a society that truly upholds the principles of liberty, equality, and the dignity and worth of all human beings. In his 1961 address he opened by describing America as an unfulfilled dream. Unlike his 1955 speech, in which he appealed to the Supreme Court and Constitution, here he claimed that the substance of this dream is rooted in the Declaration of Independence. In this founding document King could establish the first component of political service by pointing to Jefferson's acknowledgment that every human being was equal and that they all have God-given human rights. King (1986) proclaimed, "The American dream reminds us that every man is heir to the legacy of worthiness," and therefore all men should be treated with equal respect (208).

King's decision to shift the texts that provided the substance of his understanding of the American dream had several implications. First, by moving away from the Constitution to the Declaration, King was enabled to argue that the principles of freedom and equality were human rights and not simply rights that were conferred by the state. King (1986) observed, "One of the first things we notice in this dream is an amazing universalism. It does not say some men, but it says all men. It does not say all white men, but it says all men, which includes black men" (208).[2] Recall King's aforementioned claim in *Where Do We Go from Here* that when Jefferson penned the Declaration of Independence, he only intended to extend equality to white men. Therefore, it is clear that King was being consciously subversive by extending the principles of freedom and equality to black men. But King went further and claimed that it really does not matter what the founders had in mind because the American dream "says that each individual has certain basic rights that are neither conferred by nor derived from the state. To discover where they came from it is necessary to move back behind the dim mist of eternity, for they are God-given" (208).

King, by shifting to God-given rights, as opposed to Constitutional-based rights, transformed the American dream into a black freedom dream (Kelly 2002) that called for equality not only for black Americans but for all human beings no matter where in the world they resided. Consequently, King is able to establish the second component of his theory of political service by calling on Americans to cultivate a sense of love and care for all human beings, which, in turn, would motivate them to do the work necessary to transform society. King (1986) offered, "God is interested in the freedom of the whole human race and in the creation of a society where all men can live together as brothers, where every man will respect the dignity and the worth of human personality" (215). This meant that the "American dream will not become a reality devoid of a larger dream of a world of brotherhood and peace and good will" (209).

King's shift from an American dream rooted in the Constitution to one rooted in the Declaration of Independence also had implications for his notion of justice. Unlike his 1955 speech in which the American dream was the promise of equal rights held out to all American citizens, the 1961 speech stressed the democratic principles of freedom and equality. The principle-based dream provided King with a basis for a more robust, open-ended conception of justice, whereas the rights-based justification could have limited him to asking that blacks have equal protection under rights already possessed by whites; a principle-based conception of justice invited black Americans into a debate over what the application of these very principles would mean. As a result, King's thoughts on the meaning of freedom and equality continued to evolve as he became more aware of the conditions necessary for black Americans to fully flourish in American society. For instance, whereas King started off by simply calling for equality under the law, by 1962 he argued that equality meant "equality of opportunity, of privilege and property widely distributed" (King 1986, 105).

By the time King wrote his final book his views on the matter of equality and justice had grown even more. In *Where Do We Go from Here* King provided a deceptively simplistic definition of justice, which he said meant giving black Americans their due. But then King (1968b) fleshed this concept of justice out: "There is nothing abstract about this. It is as concrete as having a good job, a good education, a decent house and a share of power" (95). King knew that a call for affirmative action on behalf of black Americans would conflict with the widely held views of the American dream as—what we now refer to as—the neoliberal and the color-blind belief that America is a just society that upholds the ideal of equality of opportunity regardless of one's race; consequently, he argued that this was reason enough to discard this belief: "It is . . . important to understand that giving a man his due may often mean giving him special treatment. I am aware of the fact that this has been a troublesome concept for some liberals, since it conflicts with their traditional ideal of equal opportunity and equal treatment of people according to their individual merits. But this is a day which demands new thinking and the re-evaluation of old concepts. A society that has done something special *against* the Negro for hundreds of years must now do something special *for* him, in order to equip him to compete on a just and equal basis" (King 1968b, 95; emphasis original). King was adamant, though, that in advance of whatever new rights, privileges, and entitlements black Americans demanded be granted as a necessity to flourish, black Americans still had a responsibility to join collectively in an effort to make justice a reality for all.

Returning to the structure of King's "The American Dream" speeches, one can see that after highlighting the universalism of the American dream, he would then note America's lack of commitment to making the dream a reality. Again, King did not believe that the American creed would undoubtedly win out; therefore, he stressed the need for the third component of his theory of political service—that black Americans would have to play a central role in creating the conditions for the American dream to manifest. In his 1961 graduation speech delivered at Lincoln University the responsibility of collective action was a prominent theme in his address to the newly minted graduates. If the American dream was to come to fruition, King (1986) demanded, "We must continue to engage in creative protest in order to break down all of those barriers that make it impossible for the dream to be realized" (212–13). He cautioned against the belief that social justice would somehow roll in on the "wheels of inevitability." Instead he stressed that it will only be achieved "through the tireless effort and the persistent work of dedicated individuals" (213). King sounded a note of optimism about the results that can be achieved when black Americans discharge their responsibility: "I believe that we will be able to make a contribution as men of good will to the ongoing structure of our society and toward the realization of the American dream" (215). He then implored the graduating class to leave campus and engage in political service by becoming active participants in the struggle for justice: "And so, as you go out today, I call upon you not to be detached spectators, but involved participants, in this great drama that is taking place in our nation and around the world" (215).

Just as King's notion of justice continued to evolve, so, too, did his idea of what service would look like. According to King's 1961 "The American Dream" speech, blacks needed to engage in what he identified as "creative protest." What King had in mind was the mobilization of the masses in the form of a nonviolent protest instituted to draw attention to the plight of the least well off. However, in his 1965 "The American Dream" speech, King (1998a) had begun to call on black Americans to develop "action programs" (96). Whereas protests focus on mobilization, action programs centered on organizing black Americans in an effort to accumulate and deploy their political and economic power. In this way, King's shift from creative protests to action programs can be read as his tacit acknowledgment of the limits of his overemphasis on mobilization at the expense of organization.

To see King's shift more clearly it will be helpful to return again to his last book, *Where Do We Go from Here*. In this text, King (1968b) stressed to the black community, "Our nettlesome task is to discover how to organize our strength into compelling power so that government cannot elude our demands. We must develop, from strength, a situation in which the government finds it wise and prudent to collaborate with us" (145). Later he offered, "We must frankly acknowledge that in the past years our creativity and imagination were not employed in learning how to develop power. We found a method in nonviolent protest that worked, and we employed it enthusiastically. We did not have leisure to probe for a deeper understanding of its laws and lines of development." But ultimately, he concluded, "Although our actions were bold and crowned with successes, they were substantially improvised and spontaneous. They attained the goals set for them but carried the blemishes of our inexperience" (145). Although King is certainly highlighting some of his limitations as a leader in this passage, it must be noted that he also does not do enough to acknowledge those who *did* employ creativity and imagination in developing the community's power. For instance, students of the civil rights movement will recognize how very similar King's language is to that of community organizers such as Ella Baker, the Student Nonviolent Coordinating Committee, and other community-based organizations (For more on this point, see chapter 4).

As King's ideas about service placed more of an emphasis on organizing community power, he understood that this would require black Americans to become educated about how power worked in society. As a marginalized people, though, he believed that black Americans were "too rejected by the culture to be part of any tradition of power." For this reason, King (1968b) observed, "Necessity will draw us toward the power inherent in the creative uses of politics" (163). By encouraging black Americans to engage in a creative use of politics, King meant that they had to study the levers of power in society and challenge those sources of power with the meager means available to them. He assessed, "In our society power sources are obscure and indistinct. Yet they can always finally be traced to those forces we describe as ideological, economic and political" (146). An example of a form of creative politics in the realm of economics was the SCLC's Operation Breadbasket, which organized massive boycotts of businesses that refused to hire a proportional amount of black employees and did not invest in black-owned banks. In the case of political power, King urged blacks to exercise their right to vote and to form political organizations that would remain consistently active in supporting an agenda that secured justice for black Americans.

However, in regard to ideological power, King (1968b) acknowledged the limited influence black scholars had been able to exert on mainstream American thought through their writings alone. Rather than lament the fact, King highlighted the way in which black Americans had created an anti-elitist marriage of theory and practice. He said, "Nevertheless Negroes have illuminated imperfections in the democratic structure that were formerly only dimly perceived, and have forced a re-examination of the true meaning of American democracy." King (1968b) noted, "By taking to the streets and there giving practical lessons in democracy and its faults, Negroes have decisively influenced white thought" (146). Being shut out of traditional channels of power, "Negroes have had to write their most persuasive essays with the blunt pen of marching ranks" (147). As we can see, even though King's ideas about what service would look like continued to evolve, he never completely jettisoned the tactic of mobilization for organization. To King, service required a creative form of politics, which did not demand that blacks choose between organizing and mobilizing in order to challenge America's power structures. Rather, King firmly believed that those who were committed to justice would need both weapons at their disposal. In other words, King's shift in language signaled not a dichotomy but the continuum between the points of mobilization and organization.

King, though, was deeply aware that community organizing would mean that the black community would have to be attentive to its class divisions. In particular, he feared that the behavior and biases of the black middle class would lead them to subject working-class and impoverished black Americans to a form of secondary marginalization (Cohen 1999). Careful not to "overlook the unswerving dedication and unselfish service" of some members of the black middle class, King (1968b) excoriated those who have "forgotten their roots and are more concerned about 'conspicuous consumption' than about the cause of justice" (140). King charged, "This kind of selfish detachment has caused the masses of Negroes to feel alienated not only from white society but also from the Negro middle class" (140). Furthermore, King contended that a politics of respectability (Higginbotham 1993) had forced some in the black community to "accept middle-class prejudices toward the labor movement" (King 1968b, 151). In response, King challenged the black middle class to embrace the first component of political service by acknowledging that their lives are inextricably bound to the rest of the black community. He offered, "The relatively privileged Negro will never be what he ought to be until the underprivileged Negro is what he ought to be. The salvation of the Negro middle class is ultimately dependent upon the salvation of the Negro masses" (140–41).

The idea that the salvation of the black middle class is tied to the salvation of the rest of the black community meant that the middle class must come to value and respect the contributions to the struggle for justice made by their peers. Stating a position long held by other activists such as Baker (Ransby 2003), King (1968b) suggested, "We must involve everyone we can reach, even those with inadequate education, and together acquire political sophistication by discussion, practice and reading" (164). This would require not only that the black middle class transform their disposition toward the rest of the community but that together the entire community transform typically apolitical spaces into political classrooms. "Informal discussions and reading at home or in the streets are educational; they challenge the mind and inform our actions" (164). King realized that even if the black middle class could jettison their class and educational biases, it was more likely that pure self-interest would prevent some from heeding his call to serve themselves and others by becoming "intensive political activists" (162). Therefore, he implored, "There must be a climate of social pressure in the Negro community that scorns the Negro who will not pick up his citizenship rights and add his strength enthusiastically and voluntarily to the accumulation of power for himself and his people" (165). Perhaps no sentence better captures the goal of King's use of the American dream. By tying his vision of a more just and democratic society to his theory of political service, King was trying to create a climate of social pressure that forced his fellow Americans, especially black Americans, to take up their responsibility to serve their nation by collectively transforming themselves, others, and structures of injustice.

IV

Ultimately, it is not a coincidence that King repeatedly delivered his "The American Dream" speeches at American college campuses or that he consistently highlighted the role of the youth in many of his public addresses. King (1986) so admired the youth's commitment to service that even on the last night of his life he reemphasized how it was the youth who, by sitting in, "were really standing up for the best in the American dream" (286). King seemed to understand that the quest for justice would not be a sprint; rather, it would be a long-distance relay race. Our nation's continual struggle with structural injustice suggests that King was correct. As America's mainstream ideological thought continues to drift toward a neoliberal outlook, which seeks to thwart structural change, it is more important than ever that those who are actively resisting this shift use all of the weapons in their arsenal.

Therefore, in this chapter I have argued that more attention needs to be paid to the manner in which King conceptualized and used the rhetorical tool of the American dream. Doing so will bring about the realization that King understood the American dream as holding out the promise of a more inclusive America; one that extends the universal principles of liberty, equality, and the equal recognition of one's dignity and worth to all human beings. However, an often-overlooked component of King's conception of the American dream was his belief that this future America could only come about through collective action aimed at transforming, self, others, and structures of injustice. My claim, then, is that the radical potential of the American dream is unlocked when there is a renewed focus on this form of structure-changing collective action, which I have termed political service. Revisiting King's conception of the American dream will not only challenge attempts to divorce King's legacy from collective action but it will also restore the radical possibilities of the American dream as a political concept.

CHAPTER 3
LIFE'S FINAL COMMON DENOMINATOR

And yet they died nobly. They are the martyred heroines of a holy crusade for freedom and human dignity. And so this afternoon in a real sense they have something to say to each of us in their death . . . They say to us that we must be concerned not merely about who murdered them, but about the system, the way of life, the philosophy which produced the murderers. Their death says to us that we must work passionately and unrelentingly for the realization of the American dream.
—MARTIN LUTHER KING JR.

On August 28, 1963, Martin Luther King Jr. delivered his landmark "I Have a Dream" speech at the March on Washington for Jobs and Freedom. King began his oration by reading from carefully prepared remarks in which he explained that the marchers had descended on the nation's capital to cash a check. According to King, the Constitution and Declaration of Independence represented a promissory note that guaranteed to all Americans the rights of life, liberty, and the pursuit of happiness. Rather than honoring the promises purportedly enshrined in these founding documents, King (1986) noted, "It is obvious today that America has defaulted on this promissory note insofar as her citizens of color are concerned" (217). One hundred years after Abraham Lincoln signed the Emancipation Proclamation, King observed, "the Negro is still languishing in the corners of American society and finds himself an exile in his own land" (217). Despite King's damning indictment of the incessant oppression faced by black Americans, he remained hopeful that "somehow this situation can and will be changed." (219) The purpose of this chapter, then, is to explore the linkage between hope and political agency in King's theory of political service.

In the last chapter I argued that King repeatedly invoked the American dream as a symbol of hope with which he sought to encourage black Americans to engage in political service. For King, the importance of tethering the American dream to his theory of political service was that it connected a vision of radical possibilities with collective action aimed at transforming self, others, and structures of injustice. In contrast to the inspiration King drew from the American dream, centuries of racial oppression have produced a long train of black political thinkers for whom being a black American has meant little more than subjection to slavery, systematic oppression, and racial violence. This sentiment was succinctly captured by King's contemporary and longtime critic, Malcolm X (1965), who observed, "I don't see any American dream; I see an American nightmare" (26) More recently, Ta-Nehisi Coates, in his book *Between the World and Me* (2015), echoes Malcolm when he claims that experiencing the American dream "has never been an option" for black Americans "because the Dream rests on our backs, the bedding made from our bodies" (103). For Coates, the violence associated with the American nightmare was not mere happenstance. As he notes, "In America, it is traditional to destroy the black body—*it is heritage*" (103; emphasis original).

The tradition of destroying the black body has been captured by an onslaught of graphic accounts and videos of several unarmed black men, women, and children being shot or even suffocated to death by law enforcement officials. These police-involved killings, which rarely result in an indictment of the officers, serve as visceral confirmation that in America black lives do not matter (Taylor 2016). Against the backdrop of this systemic violence, Coates (2015) performs what has become a ritual for many black parents when he explains to his son, Samori, "And all you need to understand is that the officer carries with him the power of the American state and the weight of an American legacy, and they necessitate that of the bodies destroyed every year, some wild and disproportionate number of them will be black" (103). However unfortunate, this intergenerational ritual of preparing one's child to face the violence of the American nightmare has become a means of survival for many black Americans.

Given that systemic racial violence is often meant to extinguish po-

58 CHAPTER THREE

litical agency, one must be attentive to the way in which white racial violence is framed. For instance, political theorist Melvin Rogers (2015) highlights the potentially stultifying effects of Coates's missive to his son. Undoubtedly, the appeal of Coates's work is that he invites the reader along as he unflinchingly unveils, for Samori, the American nightmare and the racial violence that undergirds it. However, as Rogers (2015) notes, Coates may go too far by accepting "the certainty of white supremacy and its inescapable constraints." According to Rogers, the inescapability of white supremacy means that, for Coates, "white supremacy does not merely structure reality; it is reality." Possessing this outlook on the world can pose serious political challenges for contemporary black Americans who adopt it. As Rogers explains, "After all, the meaning of action is tied fundamentally to what we imagine is possible for us. But when one views white supremacy as impregnable, there is little room for one's imagination to soar and one's sense of agency is inescapably constrained." Certainly Rogers is not suggesting that contemporary black Americans should ignore the grim realities of the American nightmare. Neither is he downplaying the overwhelming sense of dread many black Americans have in the face of white racial violence. However, he is arguing that safeguarding a robust sense of political agency requires that black Americans face up to the American nightmare and its concomitant racial violence without relinquishing their sense of hope.

With this in mind, it is important to acknowledge not only the history of systemic white racial violence but also the rich tradition of gallant black Americans who preserved their sense of hope in the face of some of the bleakest expressions of the American nightmare. Nearly a fortnight after King delivered his triumphant message of hope and faith at the base of the Lincoln Memorial, he would be calling on the black community of Birmingham, Alabama, to demonstrate their deep resolve in response to white racial violence. In the months prior to the March on Washington, black Americans in Birmingham launched a campaign against segregation and economic strangulation. In retaliation to their protests, a bomb was placed in the basement of the 16th Street Baptist Church that killed four young girls—Carol Denise McNair, Cynthia Wesley, Addie Mae Collins, and Carole Robertson—as they attended Sunday school (McWhorter 2001; Garrow 2004). In 1967 King reflected on this act of terrorism by solemnly describing their murders as "the first time [he] saw that dream turn into a nightmare." Despite acknowledging the transformation of his dream into a nightmare, King (1967c) reaffirmed his faith in a better tomorrow: "Yes, I am personally the victim of deferred dreams, of blasted hopes, but in spite of that I close today by saying I still have a dream, because, you know, you can't give up in life. If you lose hope, somehow you lose that vitality that keeps life moving, you lose that courage to be, that quality that helps you go on in spite of all. And so today I still have a dream." For King, the ability to "go on in spite of all" was an essential aspect of his theory of political service. Consequently, this chapter highlights King's efforts to encourage black Americans to preserve their hope and to continue to exercise their political agency in the immediate aftermath of the bombings.

Before exploring King's response to the bombing, I will explicate what King called the third dimension of a complete life—the height. According to King, if black Americans were to transform themselves, others, and structures of injustice, in the face of the violent American nightmare, then it was imperative for them to possess robust-enough sources of strength to sustain them to "go on in spite of all." King's personal source of strength was his unshakeable belief in God. After explaining the centrality of God to King's theory of political service, I then turn to a discussion of how white Alabamans sought to systemically extinguish a sense of political agency among the black community of Birmingham. To counter these efforts, I show how King worked to subvert this logic to preserve a sense of hope and agency among Birmingham's black community. I conclude by returning to Coates's book to demonstrate alternative responses employed by contemporary black Americans to systemic white racial violence.

II

In chapter 1, I explored various iterations of King's sermon "The Three Dimensions of a Complete Life." Focusing on the first two dimensions—

the length and the breadth—I constructed King's theory of political service. I now turn to what King identified as the third dimension to give it fuller treatment in the present chapter. Recall that the first two dimensions provided the framework of King's theory of political service. However, it must be noted that King's account of human flourishing, which requires that individuals move beyond their own selfishness (length of life) by engaging in service (breadth of life) is rooted in their relation to a God figure (the height of life). King (2007) explained the relationship between humans and God in his 1954 "Dimensions" sermon thusly: "The Height of life is its reach upward toward something distinctly greater than humanity: Man must rise above earth to that great eternal reality who is the source and end of life" (154). Notice that King makes two distinct claims about God's relationship to human beings. The first is that God is the source of life and the second is that God is the end of life. Both of these claims are significant to his theory of political service, and so I will explore them in turn.

King, by claiming that God is the source of life, is asserting that God created all of humanity; thereby, God is the father, and all human beings are His children. According to King, the fact that all humans are God's children means that they are deserving of equal dignity and respect from others. The theological scholar Rufus Burrow Jr. (2006) explains the sociopolitical implications of King's conception of humanity. According to Burrow (2006), King believed that "persons are called into existence by God as free beings with the capacity to be self-determining moral agents" (173). Consequently, "If to be a person is to be free and to possess infinite, absolute dignity and worth, then persons are obligated to protest against all that undermines their humanity and dignity." He continues, "Concretely, this means that persons are always and forever obligated to take steps toward removing any obstacles to the realization of complete personhood" (Burrow 2006, 176). Since King believed that structural injustice was a means by which black Americans were stripped of both their worth and freedom—and therefore their humanity—then it follows that it is black Americans' obligation to do everything in their power to resist this pernicious form of oppression.

However, Burrow (2006) is careful to point out that there is a difference between metaphysical forms of freedom—such as freedom of will—and sociopolitical freedoms—such as the ability to choose where one lives. He cautions, "It should be remembered that metaphysical freedom does not necessarily translate into the sociopolitical freedoms that persons need in order to function fully as persons in the world" (176). The distinction between metaphysical and sociopolitical forms of freedom is important to keep in mind when interpreting King's claim that structural injustice has stripped black Americans of their freedom. He is not saying that structural injustice has dispossessed black Americans of a metaphysical form of freedom. For, if that were the case, then he could not hold black Americans culpable for failing to exercise their political agency. It is precisely because of the distinction between metaphysical and sociopolitical freedom that King (1986) can demand the following of blacks living under unjust structures: "We must make full and constructive use of the freedom we already possess. We must not wait until the day of full emancipation before we set out to make our individual and collective contributions to the life of our nation" (134). Here King is clearly stating that even if black Americans' sociopolitical freedom has been taken away, their possession of metaphysical freedom requires them to exercise their political agency by resisting their oppression.

It must be stressed that although King's account of humanity required black Americans to resist their oppression by engaging in political service, they were not the only ones obligated to do so. As Burrow (2006) points out, "In addition" to the active resistance of potential victims, King's account of humanity "means that the moral agent is obligated to act on behalf of the best interests of the moral subject who may or may not be a moral agent" (173). The upshot of King's account of humanity, then, is that white Americans were also obligated to do everything in their power to dismantle structural injustice. King, though, also knew that the intransigence of white Americans made them unreliable allies in the struggle for justice. Consequently, King's account of humanity required that black Americans love white Americans, even if they failed to discharge their responsibility to transform themselves, others, and structures of injustice.

As mentioned in chapter 1, the rigorous demand for black Americans to love their white oppressors stems from King's (2010) belief that God loves all of His children and that "*agape* is the love of God operating in the human heart . . . we love every man because God loves him" (46). King defined *agape* as "understanding and creative, redemptive goodwill for all men" (46). According to King, unlike other forms of love, *agape* is the only "love that seeks nothing in return" (45). King argued that a love that seeks nothing in return is necessary for black Americans to adopt since they could not depend on reciprocity from white Americans. In sum, King's claim that God is the source of life meant that black Americans were not only required to resist their oppression but also to love their white oppressors in the process.

The second aspect of King's discussion of the height of life is King's claim that God is the end of life. Here he was claiming that humans possess a telos to seek God. As King (2007) put it, "We were made for God and we will be restless until we find rest in him" (156). Admittedly, in King's 1954 sermon it is not clear what, if any, connection a telos to seek God has with his theory of political service. However, by his 1960s "Dimensions" sermon King began to tie the quest for justice with the quest for God. In response to a reporter who queried whether King feared the many threats made against his life in the struggle for justice, King (2007) recalled, "And I said to him, 'I have but one answer. First, I think that this cause is right. And since it is right I believe that God is with it because God is on the side of right. And therefore, I can go on with a faith that because God is with the struggle for the good life, victory is inevitable'" (404). Not only was King suggesting that when individuals seek justice they are moving ever closer to God but he was also promoting faith in God as a source for the least well off to draw on in their service to the nation.

By assuring the least well off that God was on the side of justice seekers, King meant to instill within black Americans a sense of hope that would sustain their political agency, especially in the midst of seemingly insurmountable odds. In this way, King held that if individuals placed their faith in God then they would not only have a configuration of humanity on which to cultivate an ethos of love and concern for their peers but black Americans would have the necessary resources to begin and sustain the work needed to transform structures of injustice. The need for robust resources in the battle against racial oppression may seem unimportant in the abstract. Therefore, in the next section I will lay out the conditions faced by the black community of Birmingham, Alabama, to underscore the importance of clearly defining one's source of sustenance and love of others.

III

In 1963 King was invited down to Birmingham by the Alabama Christian Movement for Human Rights. The black community of Birmingham had set out to resist the segregation and economic strangulation imposed on them from their fellow white citizens. King, then president of the SCLC, knew the campaign would be a highly volatile situation since he already witnessed the extreme violence that came along with resisting white oppression. By 1963 King had been stabbed and brutally assaulted, his house had been bombed several times, and he was subject to death threats on a daily basis. Yet, as he arrived in Birmingham he was acutely aware of the fact that he would be demanding that others also put themselves in harm's way by participating in a struggle being waged in one of the nation's most violent cities. In fact, Birmingham had become commonly referred to as "Bombingham" because of its numerous racially charged bombings. Many of these bombings took place in the Fountain Heights section where black families had moved into a predominately white neighborhood, earning it the nickname "Dynamite Hill." The most notorious of these racially charged bombings was that of the 16th Street Baptist Church (McWhorter 2001; Garrow 2004). Even though the deaths of Carol Denise, Cynthia, Addie Mae, and Carole rightfully sparked outrage across the nation, it must be understood that this bombing took place within a context of systemic intimidation meant to extinguish blacks' capacity as political agents.

For instance, Eugene "Bull" Connor, Birmingham's public safety commissioner, garnered much attention for his willingness to deploy fire hoses and police dogs on peaceful marchers. These spectacular acts of violence captured by photographers and news crews grabbed the nation's attention. However, his acts of violence were purposefully being manipulated by the leaders of the Birmingham movement. That is, it was the movement participants who instigated his violence. The public marches of "Project C" (as the campaign in Birmingham was titled, in which "C" stood for confrontation) were staged to garner as much media attention and national outrage as possible (Garrow 2004). The campaign's manipulation of the media meant that Connor's violence was, in some sense, welcomed.

Despite the fact that the organizers of Project C welcomed Connor's violence, what was perhaps most troubling about Connor was not so much the violence that he personally authorized but his turning of a blind eye to violence used by other white citizens of Birmingham. Birmingham's systemic violence against those who sought to desegregate the city was well documented. An article published as early as 1960 in the *New York Times* described how violence from extremists had silenced anyone who spoke up for desegregation, while another article in a national magazine referred to Birmingham as "A City in Fear" (as cited in Garrow 2004, 231–32). These articles demonstrate that the white populations of Birmingham adopted lethal violence as a method designed to extinguish black political agency. More pointedly, Alabama governor George Wallace, in an interview with the *New York Times* just weeks before the bombing of the 16th Street Baptist Church, succinctly captured the whites' strategy. In response to a question about blacks' attempts to exercise their political agency, Wallace replied, "What this country needs is a few first-class funerals, and some political funerals, too" (as cited in Carter 1995, 174).

Whereas King conceptualized all humans as brothers and sisters, many white Americans, like Wallace, simply did not conceptualize blacks as humans. Since black Americans were not viewed as human beings, then their lives did not have the same moral significance as their white counterparts. To clearly understand the sociopolitical implications of this conception of humanity, it is helpful to quote "Connie" Lynch at length. Lynch was a professional race baiter who made his living by offering speeches that reinforced whites' resistance to black

American equality. Speaking just days after the bombing, Lynch made the following comments at a public rally in Florida:

> Someone said, "Ain't it a shame that them little children was killed?" In the first place, they ain't little. They're fourteen or fifteen years old—old enough to have venereal diseases, and I'll be surprised if all of 'em didn't have one or more. In the second place, they weren't children. Children are little people, little human beings, and that means white people.
>
> There's little dogs and cats and apes and baboons and skunks and there's also little niggers. But they ain't children. They're just little niggers.
>
> And in the third place, it wasn't no shame they was killed. Why? Because, when I go out to kill rattlesnakes, I don't make no difference between little rattlesnakes and big rattlesnakes, because I know it is the nature of all rattlesnakes to be my enemies and to poison me if they can. So I'll kill 'em all, and if there's four less niggers tonight, then I say, "Good for whoever planted the bomb!" We're all better off . . . I believe in violence, all the violence it takes either to scare the niggers out of the country or to have 'em all six feet under. (as cited in Wade 1987, 326)[1]

Lynch's speech embodies the existential threats that both blacks and whites purportedly posed to each other from the perspective of white supremacists. According to this outlook, blacks were dangerous nonhumans whose very existence—just as that of the rattlesnake—was a threat. Consequently, it followed, that blacks needed to be exterminated.

Lynch's professed belief in violence is instructive about the aims of white violence. As Lynch says, "I believe in violence, all the violence it takes either to scare the niggers out of the country or to have 'em all six feet under." By offering two options Lynch's insatiable appetite for violence was not solely meant to be genocidal. Instead, the intent of his call for violence was largely to discourage black Americans from exercising their political agency. Taken together, Lynch's speech was part of a larger system of violence called for by the governor, condoned by the public safety commissioner, and carried out by law enforcement authorities and civilians alike. Consequently, white Alabamans positioned themselves as an existential threat to the black population of Birmingham. According to Lynch, black Americans had only two options, flee or die. It was under these systemic threats (and instances) of lethal violence that King sought to provide black Americans with a third option.

As a third option, King argued counterintuitively that the only way black Americans could effectively curb racial violence was for them to become active in the civil rights movement. That King would seek to motivate blacks to become active political agents is not at all surprising, especially as a leader in a movement predicated on citizens exercising their rights to demonstrate for what is right. What is puzzling, though, is *how* he sought to motivate them, for his tactic was to lay blame on certain members of the black community who did not attempt to resist white oppression. On the day of the 16th Street Church bombing, a reporter asked who King thought was responsible for killing the four girls. Even before a formal investigation had been completed, it was obvious that, whoever the culprit was, it was a white extremist. Anyone familiar with King's typical response to white violence would not have expected him to treat the bombing as an isolated incident. Instead, one would have expected his response to reflect that of a white attorney in Birmingham, Charles Morgan, who declared that the entire white community shared guilt for the bombing since they both tolerated and encouraged racial hatred (Branch 1988, 891). King had already made a similar argument in his "Letter from a Birmingham Jail," in which he charged that the white moderate, not the Ku Klux Klan, was the great stumbling block in the pathway to black Americans' freedom. Furthermore, King sent a telegram to Governor Wallace declaring that there was blood on Wallace's hands regarding these murders. Yet, contrary to these expectations, King publicly responded, "What murdered these four girls? The apathy and complacency of many Negroes who will sit down on their stools and do nothing and not engage in creative protest to get rid of this evil [system]" (as cited in Branch 1988, 891).[2]

The idea that King would place blame for one of the most heinous crimes perpetrated against black Americans squarely on the very victims of that violence appears to be counterproductive, if not outright disrespectful. But this interpretation is too narrow and does not consider how King utilized the threat of death to motivate black Americans to exercise their political agency. In other words, King blamed inactive blacks for the bombing, precisely because he did not think that they were doing everything in their power to, as Burrow (2006) puts it, "protest against all that undermines their humanity and dignity" (176). Recall that he was addressing a population who had the unique experience of living under conditions in which lethal violence was being used to force them to flee or die. Consequently, they experienced racial violence in a way that was potentially debilitating. This is precisely the aim of those who deploy such lethal violence; they want the dread of death to become so robust that it causes their enemies to lose all sense of agency. Understood within this context, it is clear that King was inverting the white extremist's use of the threat of death to get black Americans to retain their sense of political agency. By denying black Americans the label of powerless victim and by charging inactive blacks with the murder of the four little girls, King was seeking to preserve their sense of political agency.

To better understand King's aim, consider the logical conclusion of Lynch's speech. By declaring that blacks were not humans but rather dangerous beasts whose lives posed an existential threat to whites, Lynch was claiming that whites have every obligation to extinguish black lives. By extension, the bombing of the 16th Street Baptist Church had its own logic. White supremacists wanted blacks to know that *if* they persisted in their attempts to integrate society, *then* they would continue to be murdered. This was the exact message Wallace meant to get across when he called for a few high-class funerals, and it was one that blacks in Birmingham understood all too well. Knowing that in the aftermath of the bombing the subjection to death might possibly become debilitating for blacks, King sought to invert this logic. Instead of saying *if* blacks persisted in attempting to challenge the racial hierarchy *then* they would continue to die, he was proclaiming that *unless* blacks continued to work toward changing society, *then* they would continue to die. In other words, King's message was that blacks' efforts to challenge white Americans were not the cause of the bombing; rather, it was their lack of collective, mass resistance that had caused the deaths.

Culpability by lack of action implies capacious agency. For instance, no one would find a dog culpable for failing to do more with its life. This is because one does not typically think of dogs as agents capable of envisioning a life plan and adhering to it in any meaningful way. Therefore, by blaming blacks for the deaths of those who were murdered in the bombings, King was arguing that they possessed political agency but were failing to exercise it. He was now calling on them to become political agents, and he believed that the way to do this was to work toward transforming the unjust structures of Bombingham.

IV

Thus far I have argued that King's initial reaction to the attack was to blame inactive members of the black community for the bombing of the 16th Street Baptist Church to encourage them to exercise their political agency. However, the claim is not that in the face of such brutal violence simply assigning blame to the black community would be enough to mitigate the effects of said violence. Recognizing this fact, at the funeral for three of the four young children who were killed King drew on his theistic configuration of humanity to serve as a source of strength in the face of the imminent danger that came along with working to combat structural injustice. Just as he had in his "Dimensions" sermons, King assured the congregation that God is there for those engaged in service. What is unique about King's invocation of God during the funeral, however, is that he used the death of the four young children as evidence of God's presence in the lives of those who seek justice.

King (1986) opened his eulogy for those killed in the bombing by playing up the fact that these "unoffending; innocent and beautiful" children were the "victims of one of the most vicious, heinous crimes ever perpetrated against humanity" (221). Yet, instead of conforming to the narrative that Carol Denise, Cynthia, Addie Mae, and Carole were merely passive victims, King claimed that they "died nobly" as "martyred heroines of a holy crusade for freedom and dignity" (221). King's transition from powerless victims to active heroism in his description of those who were murdered signals his recognition that it was the young children's participation in the demonstrations that were largely responsible for breaking the back of segregation in the city. Recall that King was resisting the white supremacists' attempts to suppress black political agency. Therefore, King was arguing that death in the struggle for justice should not be taken as an indication that God had abandoned black Americans. In fact, King made the case that the young girls were agents acting on God's behalf. As he explained, "God still has a way of wringing good out of evil" (221). According to King, by dying in the midst of a battle for justice, the children's death had the potential to "lead our whole Southland from the low road of man's inhumanity to man to the high road of peace and brotherhood." He continued, "These tragic deaths may lead our nation to substitute an aristocracy of character for an aristocracy of color. The spilt blood of these innocent girls may cause the whole citizenry of Birmingham to transform the negative extremes of a dark past into the positive extremes of a bright future" (221).

King's use of such tentative language as "may" was meant to underscore the fact that his goal was to prod the entire nation into learning how to serve humanity in the manner of the young children of Birmingham. Through the actions and the deaths of Birmingham's youth, King was arguing that the youth were the agents responsible for initiating an action that could only be fully carried out if everyone else took up his or her responsibility to engage in political service (Arendt 1958). Whereas King blamed inactive black Americans for the bombing during his initial remarks, he sought to call attention to the ways in which all Americans were responsible for the bombing because of their involvement, whether tacit or explicit, in the social processes that enabled racism to flourish. He did so by shifting the blame for the deaths to the structures of injustice and away from any one individual or group. King (1986) pointed out that the young, black, political agents "have something to say to us in their death" (221). After going through a litany of various groups who might be considered blamable for the deaths, King put these aside and concluded, "They say to each of us, black and white, that we must substitute courage for caution. They say to us that we must be concerned not merely about WHO murdered them, but about the system, the way of life and the philosophy which PRODUCED the murderers." Invoking a symbol that was meant to call Americans to serve their nation by collectively working toward justice (see chapter 2), King continued, "Their death says to us that we must work passionately and unrelentingly to make the American dream a reality" (221; emphasis original).

Notice that King's eulogy for the four young girls, then, is not a complete departure from his initial response to the bombings. By positioning the young girls as political actors, King was hoping that emphasis placed on their agency would serve to mitigate the potentially debilitating effects that the threat of violence posed to the black community. Again, King was inverting the claim that these children died because they attempted to resist white oppression. Instead, King argued that these children died because their gallant actions alone cannot transform structures of injustice. Thus, King was claiming that the children had only initiated a form of political action; this meant the entire community needed to become the finishers of this action. Finishing the work the children initiated meant black Americans would need to transform themselves into political agents, transform their white peers into allies, and together transform the overall structure in which the bombing took place, for, as long as these unjust structures continued to exist, they robbed all humans of the ability to fully flourish. Consequently, King concluded that it was everyone's responsibility to collectively serve the nation by combating structural injustice.

Although King insisted that black Americans should seek to transform white Americans into allies, he was cognizant of the impact that white intransigence would have on black Americans. Quite understandably, King feared that white resistance would cause blacks to lose faith in their white peers. Therefore, King (1986) drew on his belief that God is the source of all life and implored, "We must not become bitter; nor must we harbor the desire to retaliate with violence. We must not lose faith in our white brothers. Somehow we must believe that the most misguided among them can learn to respect the dignity and worth of all human personality" (222). Despite King's call for interracial collective action, he had to come to grips with the fact that, unlike those he was addressing with his initial remarks, he was now standing before an audience of black Americans who *were* involved in the struggle for justice and who lost people they loved as a result. King felt compelled to encourage these community members to press on in the battle even if many white Americans presented themselves as uncooperative.

King, once again, called on black Americans to engage in the struggle by counterintuitively stressing that, in the end, all human beings are equally subjected to death. To understand the logic behind King's appeal, it must be understood that he was keenly aware that his audience was composed of those who felt that they were disproportionately subjected to death at the hands of white Americans. Consequently, his goal was to remind black Americans that death is not reserved just for them. King most potently made this point as he attempted to assuage the pain of those who had the most reason to resent whites—the families of the heroines. As he turned his attention to them, King commenced by admitting the great difficulty that comes along with trying to console those struck by tragedy. However, instead of soothing the families by offering them pleasant platitudes, he emphasized that all humans must die. King (1986) remarked, "May I now say a word to you, the members of the bereaved families. It is almost impossible to say anything that can console you at this difficult hour and remove the deep clouds of disappointment which are floating in your mental skies. But I hope you can find a little consolation from the universality of this experience. Death comes to every individual. There is an amazing democracy about death. It is not aristocracy for some of the people, but a democracy for all of the people. Kings die and beggars die; rich men die and poor men die; old people die and young people die; death comes to the innocent and it comes to the guilty. Death is the irreducible common denominator of all men" (222). Notice that by stressing that all human beings are equally subjected to death, King was trying to encourage the family members to remain committed to the struggle for justice by highlighting that whites must ultimately die as well. In other words, he was rebuffing the white extremists' logic, which pointed to the deaths of the four young girls as evidence that white Americans possessed dominion over blacks' lives.

In fact, King was arguing that whites do not even possess complete dominion over their own lives. Instead, King articulated his belief that ultimately God is the only being with dominion over human life.

Rather than being the end, King explained to those in attendance that for Christians death is "an open door which leads man into life eternal" (King 1986, 222). Drawing on his belief that to seek God is in the human telos, King implored, "Let this daring faith, this great invincible surmise, be your sustaining power during these trying days." Certainly, many of those attending the funeral agreed with King that life is "as hard as crucible steel." However, he reminded them, "Through it all, God walks with us. Never forget that God is able to lift you from fatigue of despair to the buoyancy of hope, and transform dark and desolate valleys into sunlit paths of inner peace" (222). In other words, King called on the parishioners to reject the fear that the white supremacists were attempting to dole out and to instead know that if they would only seek God by standing up and resisting white oppression, then God would sustain them in their struggle for justice against the most overwhelming odds.

V

I want to conclude this chapter by returning to Coates's book *Between the World and Me*. Despite Coates's implicit and explicit critiques of King, I argue that he inadvertently captures much of King's message about hope and political agency in the face of the American nightmare. This is because Coates provides the reader with two very different responses that contemporary black Americans can have to systemic racial violence. One response is that of Coates, who, although he encourages black Americans to struggle, does so while simultaneously foreclosing the possibility that they can resist white supremacy in any meaningful way.

One particular moment that epitomizes Coates's response to systemic racial violence comes very early in his book. After the breaking news that Darren Wilson, the white police officer who shot and killed a black teenager, Michael Brown, would not be indicted, Coates tells the reader about his inability to console his crying son. Coates (2015) explains to Samori, "I did not tell you that it would be okay, because I have never believed it would be okay" (11). Perhaps it is understandable that Coates was unable to tell his son that white supremacy would forever be eradicated and things will soon be better. However, within Coates's larger worldview, his inability to console his son has deeper sociopolitical implications. As Rogers (2015) explains, "Forget telling his son it *will* be okay. Coates cannot even tell him that it *may* be okay. 'The struggle is really all I have for you,' he tells his son, 'because it is the only portion of this world under your control.' What a strange form of control. Black folks may control their place in the battle, but never with the possibility that they, and in turn their country to which they belong, may win" (emphasis original). Without any sense of hope that black Americans can achieve sociopolitical freedom, Coates seems to suggest that blacks should seek a form of apolitical, psychological freedom. By rejecting "magic in all its forms," Coates (2015) insists that he was freed to consider the "question of how one should live within the black body, within a country lost in the Dream" (12). Ultimately, Coates concludes that the question is unanswerable but not futile. As he explains, "The greatest reward of this constant interrogation, of confrontation with the brutality of my country, is that it has freed me from ghosts and girded me against the sheer terror of disembodiment" (12). Unfortunately, it is unclear what the upshot of Coates's idea of confrontation is. This leads Cornel West (2017) to conclude, "For Coates, defiance is narrowly aesthetic—a personal commitment to writing with no connection to collective action."

Coates acknowledges that he reaches these dour conclusions about the role of hope in the black struggle, in part because of his configuration of humanity. In fact, on several occasions throughout the text he implicitly, and explicitly, rebuffs King and his Christian configuration of humanity. For instance, King's (1986) configuration of humanity enabled him to steadfastly affirm: "The arc of the moral universe is long, but it bends toward justice" (252). In contrast, Coates (2015) asserts, "And so I had no sense that any just God was on my side. 'The meek shall inherit the earth' meant nothing to me. The meek were battered in West Baltimore, stomped out at Walbrook Junction, bashed up on

Park Heights, and raped in the showers of the city jail. My understanding of the universe was physical, and its moral arc bent toward chaos then concluded in a box" (28). Thus, black Americans cannot subvert the logic of white supremacy within Coates's configuration of humanity because it is a natural force that cannot be contained. In the wake of another police shooting, which took the life of Coates's friend, Prince Jones, Coates observes the following about white racial violence: "The earthquake cannot be subpoenaed. The typhoon will not bend under indictment." According to Coates, Prince Jones's killer "was a force of nature, the helpless agent of our world's physical laws (83).

   In contrast to Coates, King believed that he could subvert the logic of white supremacists since, in his configuration of humanity, whites do not have supreme dominion over the black body. For instance, King also talked about natural disasters but in a profoundly different manner than does Coates. In his eulogy for the bombing victims King said to the family of the aggrieved, "Like the ever-flowing waters of the river, life has its moments of drought and its moments of flood" (King 1986, 222). By likening encounters with vicious white supremacy—like that which his audience was currently enduring—as moments, rather than a fixed state of affairs, King sought to dispel any sense that white supremacy is an everlasting certainty in this world. He underscored this claim by next observing, "Like the ever-changing cycle of the seasons, life has the soothing warmth of its summers and the piercing chill of its winters" (222). To be clear, King did not think that black Americans needed to stand pat and wait for their conditions to change like the seasons. Instead, he argued that real change can only come about if, and only if, black Americans persevered "in spite of all," and committed to engaging in political service.

   As we near the fifty-year anniversary of King's assassination, it is reasonable to query whether King's beliefs are outdated relics of a woebegone period. Perhaps it is unreasonable to expect black Americans to continue to remain hopeful and steadfast in the struggle against white racial violence. As a parent of a black child, Coates has to live with the paralyzing fear that his son will also fall prey to black disembodiment. Maybe it is too much to expect contemporary black parents to be anything but pessimistic about the prospects of defeating white supremacy and crippled by the fear it engenders. Except that several times in *Between the World and Me*, Coates finds himself very much at odds with other black parents who have lost a child to white racial violence. While Coates stops short of dismissing these parents altogether, he does draw sharp distinctions between how he responds to the deaths of their sons and the way in which the parents have responded.

At one point in his text Coates (2015) tells his readers about a conversation between him, his son, and the mother of a young black teenager who was killed by a white man for playing his music too loud. "I told her that the idea that someone on that jury thought it plausible there was a gun in the car baffled the mind. She said that she was baffled too, and that I should not mistake her calm probing for the absence of anger. *But God had focused her anger away from revenge and toward redemption, she said. God had spoken to her and committed her to a new activism"* (113; emphasis added). In this mother's response we see a contemporary example of what type of action King sought to motivate among black Americans who encounter white racial violence. Rather than capitulate to the agency-robbing effects of white supremacy, this mother of a slain teen drew on her relationship to God to transform herself, seek the transformation of others in the form of redemption, and push through her grief and anger to challenge structures of white supremacy.

At another point in the text Coates (2015) describes the little that he can recall from Prince Jones's funeral. He recounts, "What I remember is all the people who spoke of Prince's religious zeal, his abiding belief that Jesus was with him . . . I remember Dr. Mabel Jones, Prince's mother, speaking of her son's death as a call to move from her comfortable suburban life into activism. I heard several people ask for forgiveness for the officer who'd shot Prince Jones down" (78). Strikingly, those who spoke at Jones's funeral had a similar response to the aforementioned mother of the slain teenager. In both instances there existed a personal connection to God, which compelled the black Americans to transform themselves into people who believe in forgiveness and the redemption of others and to channel their loss into political activism. Although these orators appear to be speaking sincerely of life-altering changes that have

enlisted them in the battle against white oppression, Coates sardoni-
cally dismisses their proclamations as mere "rituals." He notes, "I only
vaguely recall my impressions of all of this. But I know that I have always
felt great distance from the grieving rituals of my people, and I must
have felt it powerfully then" (78).

Coates (2015) explains that part of the divide between him and those
engaged in the ritual of grieving was his "rejection of a Christian God,"
which caused him to "see no higher purpose in Prince's death" (79). The
objective of this chapter is not to suggest that all contemporary black
Americans need to believe in a Christian God. Rather, in addition to exploring the linkage between hope and agency in King's theory of political service, the goal has been to highlight the dangers of not having sufficient resources to sustain contemporary black Americans in the long
and arduous battle against structural injustice. These resources may
come in any number of different forms—psychological, emotional, or
spiritual—the point is that they need to generate a sense of hope that exercising collective political agency can make a difference. Without sufficient resources, black Americans may spiral into a sense of fatalism,
which can make even the most basic generative practices nearly impossible. As a cautionary note, I will conclude with the rest of the exchange
between Coates, Samori, and the mother of the slain teenager. Coates
(2015) says, "Then the mother of the murdered boy rose, turned to you,
and said, 'You exist. You matter. You have value. You have every right to
wear a hoodie, to play your music as loud as you want. You have every
right to be you. And no one should deter you from being you. You have
to be you. And you can never be afraid to be you." He continues, "I was
glad she said this. I have tried to say the same to you, and if I have not
said it with the same direction and clarity, I confess that is because I am
afraid. And I have no God to hold me up" (113). It seems unlikely that
young black Americans, like Samori, will be able to continue to struggle against white oppression if their parents do not even possess the resources to tell them that they matter and have value.

CHAPTER 4
A CALL TO CONSCIENCE

Here is the true meaning and value of compassion and nonviolence when
it helps us to see the enemy's point of view, to hear his questions, to know
his assessment of ourselves. For from his view we may indeed see the basic
weaknesses of our own condition, and if we are mature, we may learn and grow
and profit from the wisdom of the brothers who are called the opposition.
—MARTIN LUTHER KING JR.

I

In an essay published posthumously, Martin Luther King Jr. encouraged white Americans to join the civil rights movement but cautioned
that they should do so in a humble manner. He observed that many
white Americans "joined our movement with a kind of messianic faith
that they were going to save the Negro and solve all of his problems very
quickly." He claimed that white Americans tended to be "aggressive and
insensitive to the opinions and abilities of the black people with whom
they were working; this has been especially true of students" (King 1986,
316). King explained that these young people possessed a form of "white
paternalism" that prevented them from knowing "how to work in a supporting, secondary role" (316). Although King's observations are about
potential white allies, they bear an important lesson for all who seek to
engage in political service. Namely, that even well-intentioned collective action can be undermined if individuals do not recognize their own
fallibility, limitations, and shortsightedness. Consequently, rather than
empowering members of the black community, King charged that the
white students further exasperated their feelings of "black inferiority"
(316).

The idea that King could accuse anyone else of possessing a "messianic faith" or of being "aggressive and insensitive to the opinions and abilities" of others may seem laughable to his critics. Despite being lauded by peers such as A. Philip Randolph, who once anointed him "the moral leader of our nation" (as quoted in Sitkoff 2008, 121), King's detractors were critical of both his public leadership and his personal morality. For example, members of the black youth movement often mockingly referred to King as "de Lawd" because of his penchant to draw comparisons between himself and Jesus Christ when avoiding dangerous campaigns such as the Freedom Rides (Branch 1988, 467).[1] Also, political activist and thinker—and the SCLC's first full-time employee—Ella Baker, chided King for his top-down leadership and his tendency to hover above community members rather than embed himself within their day-to-day realities (Ransby 2003). In addition to King's many shortcomings as a leader of a public movement, his private indiscretions have also been well documented. As Michael Eric Dyson (2000) points out, "At times, King was personally reckless, even dangerously so" (5).

Today King's public leadership and personal morality remain a political football among contemporary Americans. For instance, religious studies scholar Michael G. Long recently made headlines when he claimed, "Dr. King never publicly welcomed gays at the front gate of his beloved community. But he did leave behind a key for them—his belief that each person is sacred, free and equal to all . . . others" (as qtd. in Blake 2012). Meanwhile, others argue that King's activism for democratic inclusion was tempered by his Christian commitments. This is exemplified by Bernice King's suggestion that her father "did not take a bullet for same-sex marriage" (as qtd. in Blake 2012). These opposing positions point to an apparent contradiction within King's Christian beliefs. In one sense, his interpretation of Christianity provides the basis for his theory of political service, which champions social justice for the oppressed. Yet, it also appears to reinforce patriarchy, heteronormativity, and other potentially oppressive norms.

Despite King's shortcomings as a leader and his purported sexism, homophobia, and many other problematic views, Dyson (2000) cautions, "We do not have to make him a saint to appreciate his greatness. Neither should we deny his imperfections as we struggle to remember and reactivate his legacy" (5). Agreeing with both Dyson and King's critics, I contend that it is important not to shield King from criticism over his messianic tendencies and plethora of other shortcomings. However, I also stress that there is value in exploring how he publicly worked through these inadequacies. To be clear, the purpose of this chapter is not to delve into the salacious details of King's personal life. Nor will I attempt to adjudicate King's position on contemporary civil rights issues. Instead, the focus of this chapter is to point to those moments in King's writings and speeches when he openly acknowledges his fallibility, and, consequently, his responsibility to correct his previous outlooks and future courses of action. While examining moments in which King performs a public assessment of his shortcomings will not excuse them, they can be instructive about how we may come to grips with our own fallibility.

King's beliefs about fallibility, I argue, were rooted in his understanding of the gulf between sin and salvation. According to King, all human beings are sinners who are unable to achieve a status of complete salvation. If a human could achieve complete salvation, then he or she would become a saint, who is without fault and is therefore defined over and against an "other"—a sinner. However, as King (2007) observed, "the saint always recognizes that he's a sinner, and the worst sinner in the world is the man who feels that he isn't a sinner. That is the point at which he's the greatest sinner" (386). King believed that the reality of the human condition meant that no human is without fault and, therefore, it is imperative that all humans acknowledge their own fallibility. Beginning with the premise of human fallibility, King sought to cultivate a sense of compassionate humility, which he hoped would create a space for listening to others, acceptance of one's shortcomings, and, ultimately, a change in one's thoughts and actions. For King, the cultivation of these sensibilities and practices is a necessary component of political service, for it ensures that we can serve in a manner that is respectful and sensitive to the opinions and abilities of others. In what follows I briefly discuss King's understanding of sin and salvation and its polit-

ical salience. I then explore two moments in King's life when he publicly acknowledged his own fallibility, owned up to his shortcomings,
and changed his course of action. The first instance I explore is King's
decision to shift from a singular emphasis on political mobilization to
a call for a more concerted effort at political organization. The other instance examined is King's decision to speak out against the war in Vietnam. Taken together, these moments provide examples of the sensibilities and practices underlying King's theory of political service, which
may be instructive for those engaging in contemporary struggles for justice.

‖

In the last chapter I explored how King encouraged black Americans to
preserve their sense of hope and political agency by providing a close
reading of King's eulogy for three of the four young children who were
murdered in the bombing of Birmingham, Alabama's, 16th Street Baptist
Church. Despite the many admirable facets of King's sermon, one could
also argue that his eulogy is, in part, an example of the cloak of holiness
that many Christians adorn to form a wall of separation between them
and those they deem as sinners. This is because King (1986) ends his remarks by offering the following about the nature of the young children's
death: "Where they died and what they were doing when death came
will remain a marvelous tribute to each of you and an eternal epitaph
to each of them. They died not in a den or dive nor were they hearing or
telling filthy jokes at the time of their death. They died within the sacred
walls of the church after discussing a principle as eternal as love" (223).
King's laudatory description of where the young girls died and what
they were discussing at the time of their deaths was meant to confirm
that their lives held tremendous value because they were good and re-
spectable members of the black race. By contrasting the circumstances
under which the children died to that of a dive or a den, King was edify-
ing the best attributes of black Americans while implicitly policing the
behavior of those who fell outside of the community's acceptable norms
(Carby 1992; Cohen 1999). King's eulogy seems to imply that if the chil-

dren had died in a less reputable location, then their lives would have held less value, would be condemnable, and would not be a "marvelous tribute" to the black community.

Political theorist George Shulman (2008) argues that this is symptomatic of a troubling by-product of King's Christian beliefs. To be clear, Shulman recognizes that King invokes a prophetic form of Christianity, which encourages the oppressed to become agents in their struggle against domination. However, he also expresses some wariness about King's tendency to "moralize politics" and black agency in ways that are problematic (106). According to Shulman, King's moralization of politics required that the "sinner" seek a form of salvation that was found in his trope of rebirth, "which posits a *pure* condition to be reached; an 'after' that redeems an injured, subordinated, impure 'before'; and a 'higher' that redeems a 'lower' of particularity, aggression, desire—of sin" (128). By naming certain actions as sin, and therefore certain actors as sinners, King seemingly contributes to the divisions between groups of people by defining one's identity over and against an "other" who was labeled a sinner and who therefore needed to be purified.

Shulman (2008) contrasts King's understanding of sin and salvation with that of James Baldwin, of whom he says, "Baldwin also speaks of redemption, but not of rebirth. We do not *purify* ourselves of corruption (by sinful impulses, unjust conduct, or idolatrous culture) to *recover* a prior purity, first principles, or a lost revolutionary treasure." He goes on to claim, "Rebirth implies transcending a historical embodiment at once carnal and social, whereas redemption for Baldwin is (generated by) 'accepting' (*wrestling with* rather than *purifying*) our incompletion and abiding need for others, our willful partiality toward them and obscurity to ourselves, our suffering as embodied, mortal, historical beings" (133; emphasis original). According to Shulman, Baldwin encourages acceptance of the human condition, while King teaches that we must seek a salvation that can be attained by overcoming our corrupt human nature. As evidence of King's drive to subordinate his carnal desires, Shulman claims that King closets his sexual life. "For he is a *prophet* who lives and dies for the *redemption* of human desire in the love of the other; his office and persona require him to embody the righteousness that elevates the base into the sublime, the carnal into the moral." Consequently, King cannot confess his carnal desires because "impurity discredits the authority of the prophet by reducing him to un-redeemed particularity" (133). Ultimately, in the struggle against white oppression, not only is King forced to police the unsavory behaviors of others but he must first, and foremost, police his own public image. Since, as Shulman explains, "Such unmasking also subverts King's po-litical project by staining the redemptive universalism he (and blacks) must exemplify" (133).

Shulman is correct that King discussed sin as a personal transgres-sion that one must seek to overcome. As King biographer David J. Gar-row (2004) notes, "King's behavior stood at a great distance from his professed beliefs about sexuality, and the contradictions created pain-ful and at times overwhelming guilt" (376). Rather than openly embrac-ing his sin, Harvard Sitkoff (2008) suggests that King "often made a kind of public confessional the subtext of his sermons" (129). These confes-sionals began to increase as King's stature continued to rise within the civil rights movement. Once, in an attempt to blackmail King, the FBI sent a package to his home with audio recordings of King engaged in several extramarital affairs. In a sermon that King delivered around this time he told his Ebenezer Baptist Church congregation, "Each of us is two selves, and the great burden of life is to always try to keep the higher self in command. Don't let the lower self take over . . . Every now and then you'll be unfaithful to those that you should be faithful to" (as qtd. in Garrow 2004, 376). To Shulman's point, King's political project dis-allowed him to fully unmask his carnal indulgences; instead, King im-plored his congregants, and more importantly, himself, to strive toward overcoming these sinful desires. King's anxiety-induced sermon aside, within the larger corpus of his works his conception of sin was far more complex. In fact, as I demonstrate, King's thoughts on sin and salvation more closely resembled Baldwin's notion of rebirth than Shulman ac-knowledges.

The complexity of King's ideas on sin and salvation can be seen in one of his early sermons titled "Man's Sin and God's Grace."[2] Here King (2007) unequivocally declared, "Man is a sinner before the Almighty

God. That is one of the basic facts of the universe and one of the basic facts of life" (382). According to King, as modern man became more enlightened he attempted to discard the idea that he was indeed a sinner. He explained, "[Christian liberalism] fell victim to the danger that forever confronts any new view, and that is that it became sentimental and soft, feeling that man was evolving from a lower state to a higher state and eventually he would move on up the evolutionary ladder and throw off all of the evils and sin of his nature. Then, we came back to see that even after all of that man is still a sinner" (382). Whereas King, at times, used the language of "lower" and "higher" to suppress his carnal desires, here he uses the same language to highlight a flaw of Christian liberalism. According to King, no human can reach a purified state in which he or she will completely overcome sin. King openly acknowledged that he was no exception to this rule. He confessed, "We all have a private self that we don't want the public self to discover" (384). More pointedly, he volunteered, "I don't know about you, but when I look at myself hard enough and deep enough and go on back from my public self to my private self, I don't feel like crying out with the Pharisee, 'I thank Thee, God, that I'm not like other men.' But I find myself saying, 'Lord, be merciful unto me a sinner.' There is that dimension which runs the gamut of human life so that man in his personal experiences discovers this tragic dimension and this awful tendency of sin" (386). For King, like Baldwin, the first step in the process of human redemption is acceptance of the fact that all humans are sinners and that this condition cannot ever be overcome.

As King often does in his thinking, he stressed that it is imperative to move the issue beyond the individual realm and to focus on the larger social processes in which all human beings are involved. Citing Reinhold Niebuhr (1932), King (2007) explained, "But you know this thing of sin grows even worse when we go out to the social dimensions of it, when we pass from the person to the social" (386). Given King's belief that we all are incomplete and are therefore dependent on others to flourish, he acknowledged that we will never be able to evade society and thus be without sin. King summed up his understanding of the interplay between sin, society, and the human condition thusly, "Man can never escape evil in his life. He is a part of the structure of society and so he must be a part of all the greed in society, he's a part of all the wars of society, and even if he's a pacifist, he's still contributing to the very thing that he's revolting against. This is the tragedy of collective and social life—that man *never* gets out of sin because he's caught up in society, and he can't get out of society because if he got out of that he wouldn't be man" (387; emphasis original). At one point in the sermon King paused to acknowledge that he was perhaps being too moribund in his description of the human condition. Rather than going back on his claims, he further embraced Niebuhr by declaring Christianity, "the most pessimistic religion in the world, for it recognizes the tragic and awful dimensions of man's sin" (387). However, as was discussed in the last chapter, King always balanced his sober assessment of the human condition with an unwavering sense of hope. Thus, he goes on to proclaim that Christianity is also "the most optimistic religion in the world, for it recognizes the heightening dimensions of God's grace and how God's grace can come in and pick up" (387).

According to King, humans do not receive God's grace by becoming purified. Instead, King (2007) maintained that humans could never overcome their sinfulness; therefore grace is something humans receive from God but "don't merit" and "don't deserve" (387). Given the human condition, King believed that there is forever a gulf between humanity's sinful nature and complete salvation. In a sermon delivered only a month before his death, King (1998a) explained, "Salvation isn't reaching the destination of absolute morality, but it's being in the process and on the right road" (196). By declaring that salvation is not a final destination, King, in this aptly titled sermon, "Unfulfilled Dreams," was encouraging his congregants to acknowledge the fact that they will never overcome their sinful nature, and therefore must accept their incompletion.

Given King's thoughts on sin and salvation, he knew that he would have been the "greatest sinner" had he continued to mask his sins. However, King came to the realization that exemplifying the possibility of redemption meant looking within and affirming that one is not above the weaknesses that define the human condition. Consequently, King openly embraced his sinfulness in an act of unity with others. "I don't know this morning about you, but I can make a testimony. You don't need to go out this morning saying that Martin Luther King is a saint. Oh, no. I want you to know this morning that I'm a sinner like all of God's children. But I want to be a good man" (King 1998a, 198). It's important to note that, just like salvation, being a "good man" did not mean having reached a purified destination; instead, it simply meant being on the right road. Ultimately, King argued that salvation is a process predicated on acceptance of one's fallibility and the need to foster a sense of openness and compassion for others, who are equally as fallible.

III

Although King's conceptions of sin and salvation are rooted in his Christian beliefs, they have implications for his larger political project. Applied more broadly, King's conception of sin and salvation informed his beliefs about human fallibility. This is because rather than viewing the world between the prism of saints and sinners, individuals are prodded to recognize that all humans are flawed. If individuals could accept their own fallibility, King thought, then this realization could be leveraged to cultivate the appropriate sensibilities and practices conducive to building a progressive political coalition. To be clear, King's views on fallibility and receptivity were not novel; they were actually a longstanding cornerstone of Ella Baker's approach to political organizing.

Consider Charles M. Payne's (1989) discussion of Baker's thoughts on dealing with difference within political collectives. Payne queries, "How shall we deal with the differences and disagreements among ourselves, real or imagined, without alienating one another?" (895). He observes that this question is an important but underappreciated aspect of Baker's thinking on social change. He explains, "Products of the society we wish to change, we carry within ourselves some of its worse tendencies, including tendencies that will lead to self-aggrandizing and exploitative relationships. Once, in the context of an argument within SNCC [Student Nonviolent Coordinating Committee] over who had the right to participate in the movement, Baker said, 'We need to penetrate the mystery of life and perfect the mastery of life and the latter requires understanding that human beings are human beings.'" Payne continues, "Unless we do a better job of responding to the human contradictions and weaknesses of the people we work with, we are likely to continue to create politics that are progressive in the ideas expressed but disempowering in the way individuals expressing those ideas relate to one another" (896). According to Payne, Baker recognized that humans can never fully immunize themselves from the worst aspects of society and that this was simply a fact of the human condition. Accordingly, Baker sought to cultivate an ethos among the members of SNCC that was responsive to difference by recognizing that the contradictions and weaknesses found in others also existed within every individual. Thus, the process of overcoming differences and disagreements begins with first recognizing one's own shortcomings and inadequacies. Through this process, one can humbly and compassionately engage others, which opens up space to hear their opinions and even their criticisms of ourselves. As Payne points out, without taking these steps, the members of SNCC ran the risk of replicating the domineering power dynamics exhibited by the "messianic faith" of the white student volunteers.

The convergence between King and Baker is an underappreciated aspect of King's political thought. In recent years, scholars have increasingly placed King into conversation with Baker. The pairing of King and Baker is usually done to highlight their contrasting approaches to leadership and political strategies. In these accounts Baker is often held up as a champion of the empowerment of everyday citizens because of her emphasis on the hard work of embedding oneself in a local community and organizing its citizens to realize their own leadership potential. Meanwhile, King is often portrayed as a great rhetorician who possesses the unique skill of mobilizing masses to protest an unjust cause (Ransby 2003; Coles 2008; Hauerwas and Coles 2008). However, King's penchant for mobilization, his critics charge, worked to effectively perpetuate his status as a leader in the civil rights movement but did very little to actually empower citizens to effect political change. This is especially true, they claim, once the protests aimed at attracting national attention died down and he inevitably abandoned their local struggle

(Carson 2005). Therefore, Baker has come to be seen as the model of grassroots, group-centered leadership, whereas King is represented as an example of top-down, singular leadership.

One such critic of King's privileging of mobilization at the expense of organization is political theorist Romand Coles. According to Coles (2008), as a Baptist preacher King participated in the long-time tradition of "call and response." In this practice the pastor calls out from the pulpit to the parishioners in such a way that moves them "into listening, understanding, seeing, and acting toward a better future" (46). To be clear, Coles does not oppose King's advocacy of mobilization as an approach to affect political change. Rather, Coles's main claim is that although King called on others to become political actors, he was "insufficiently attentive" to the daily practices of "cultivating selves and communities" that place an emphasis on "listening in the development of ethical and political relationships." Coles calls this emphasis on listening "response and call" and argues that it was central to Baker's vision of organizing (44).

The ability to listen, according to Coles, was symptomatic of a general receptivity to experience that Baker sought to cultivate among organizers that she taught. Says Coles, "One of her chief objectives was to participate in building an organization in which teachers would above all 'teach their capacity to learn,' and leaders would aim to engender more leaders" (Hauerwas and Coles 2008, 63). Toward this end, Baker stressed the importance of "developing a practiced culture of people with discerning eyes and ears for present-yet-subordinated possibilities in self, others, and the surrounding world" (63). Essentially, Coles's criticism of King's embracement of political mobilization is really a critique of King's overemphasis on one's voice at the expense of doing the important work of cultivating the leadership capacity of others through listening. Coles claims that even though King was calling on Americans to engage in the work necessary to make America more just and democratic, his "words began too often to fall upon people who, for lack of practice, were insufficiently resonant to give energetic, reflective, active, and durable responses" (63).

There is no gainsaying that King's tenure as president of the SCLC was primarily marked by the adoption of large-scale mobilizing efforts. Toward the end of his life, though, King began to place a greater emphasis on the organizing tradition. Coles, in a footnote, acknowledges King's shift. He observes, "Of course, in the mid-1960s King moved more and more toward efforts at deep democratic grassroots organizing" (Hauerwas and Coles 2008, 56n25). However, this positive acknowledgment of King's progress is followed by a stern critique of King:

Perhaps the extent to which he too weakly grasped the practices of church and community traditions, with which Baker was imbued and from which he might have learned and employed a great deal, can be assessed in his late book *Where Do We Go From Here: Chaos or Community?* When elaborating upon the imperative that blacks "need to become intense political activists," King employs the example of the tradition of Jewish social action in the United States. While he is right that this is a rich tradition, and strategically correct to affirm the alliance with Jews by use of their example here, it is striking that there is no mention of the practices of the black church life, nor any of the black radical-democratic tradition in Harlem and elsewhere. He would have had to tap deeper into these historical currents of wisdom, relationship, and action to proceed down the paths he nevertheless so brilliantly evoked. (56)

In this passage Coles states that even when King finally came around to understanding the importance of organizing, he failed to acknowledge the rich organizing tradition within the black community. However, if we examine the fuller context of the chapter from which Coles draws in his discussion of King, I believe we will gain both a different perspective about what King was up to and a greater appreciation for his capacity to model his fallibility and compassionately listen to others.

As I stated at the outset, King committed a plethora of political missteps, led failed campaigns, had personal flaws, and let many people down throughout his lifetime. Some of King's most vociferous detractors were members of the black youth movement who—in part due to the influence of Baker—were deeply skeptical of King's penchant for mobilizing the masses at the expense of engaging in the daily practices that empowered communities. The impact of their criticisms on King can be seen throughout the fifth chapter of *Where Do We Go from Here?* For it is here that King began to signal a shift in strategy by moving beyond a singular focus on mobilization toward more of an emphasis on community organizing. However, as Coles notes, the black community already had a longstanding commitment to the organizing tradition. In contrast to Coles's assertion that King is failing to acknowledge the longstanding tradition of organizing in the black community, I argue that King was publicly admitting his fallibility by acknowledging that he had been insufficiently attentive to the organizing tradition in the past. In other words, my claim is that King was signaling not only that he had heard the criticisms voiced by others but that he had compassionately listened to his interlocutors and was prepared to correct his course of action.

King's tactical shift toward political organizing can be seen at the very outset of the fifth chapter. King (1968b) opens by striking a tone eerily similar to that of one of his fiercest critics, Kwame Ture, when he opines, "[The Black community's] nettlesome task is to discover how to organize our strength into compelling power so that government cannot elude our demands. We must develop, from strength, a situation in which the government finds it wise and prudent to collaborate with us" (145). However, not only did King embrace the language of Black Power advocates he also acknowledged the limitations of his past practices. King (1968b), speaking about his own failed leadership, confessed, "We must frankly acknowledge that in the past years our creativity and imagination were not employed in learning how to develop power. We found a method in nonviolent protest that worked, and we employed it enthusiastically" (145). King only offered a tepid defense of these shortcomings, "We did not have leisure to probe for a deeper understanding of its laws and lines of development." He then pulled back the curtain to reveal his faults to the reader: "Although our actions were bold and crowned with successes, they were substantially improvised and spontaneous. They attained the goals set for them but carried the blemishes of our inexperience" (145). Further underscoring his own fallibility, "De Lawd" went on to denude himself of any pretense of omniscience: "None of us can pretend that he knows all the answers" (145).

King, having publicly acknowledged his fallibility and his ability to humble himself in an effort to build a progressive coalition with others, continued to reinforce this message throughout the remainder of the chapter. In the realm of economics, King highlighted the work that the SCLC's Operation Breadbasket was doing in putting pressure on local corporations to hire blacks and to invest their money in black-owned banks. In addition to these efforts, he also proposed a "coalition of an energized section of labor, Negroes, unemployed and welfare recipients" (King 1968b, 150). King believed that this coalition had the potential to push forth major economic and social reforms, but he cautioned that it could only work if the black community relinquished its stigmatization of labor jobs. King observed that a bias had developed among all classes of black Americans that promoted professional jobs and denigrated labor jobs. He said, "We allowed ourselves to accept middle-class prejudices toward the labor movement. Yet this is one of those fields in which higher education is not a requirement for high office. In shunning it, we have lost an opportunity" (151). Here King was not asking the black community to strive for less but rather to recognize that there is dignity in all labor. He held that unless the black community was able to rid themselves of their biases against labor jobs they would not be able to forge a strong coalition between class lines.

Turning to the realm of politics, King named three forms of weaknesses he felt prohibited black Americans from shoring up their political power. Echoing W. E. B. Du Bois's (1903) critique of Booker T. Washington (especially chapter 3), King identified the first weakness as the lack of genuine support for black leaders among the black masses. He noted, "Although genuinely popular leaders are now emerging, most are selected by white leadership, elevated to position, supplied with resources and inevitably subjected to white control." This, in turn, causes the masses to be suspicious of their black leaders. "The Negro politician they know spends little time in persuading them that he embodies personal integrity, commitment and ability; he offers few programs and less service" (King 1968b, 156). As a remedy to this crisis in leadership King called on the masses to "create leaders who embody virtues we can respect, who have moral and ethical principles we can applaud with an enthusiasm that enables us to rally support for them based on confidence and trust." King indicated that the black masses create principled leaders when they "demand high standards and give consistent, loyal support to those who merit it" (158). In other words, King was calling on the people to exercise their vote and their voice in holding their political leaders more accountable.

Although King was urging the masses to exercise their democratic voice, he also wanted to emphasize the need for humble listening by black leaders. After acknowledging that some criticisms of black leaders can be overblown, King (1968b) admitted that they are often deserved. He pronounced, "The most serious is aloofness and absence of faith in their people" (168). Just as he had listened to the critics in the youth movement and rendered himself vulnerable before them, he was teaching other leaders to listen humbly and courageously to their own constituencies. To emphasize the importance of listening to good leadership, King told a little story that bears repeating: "I learned a lesson many years ago from a report of two men who flew to Atlanta to confer with a civil rights leader at the airport. Before they could begin to talk, the porter sweeping the floor drew the local leader aside to talk about a matter that troubled him. After fifteen minutes had passed, one of the visitors said bitterly to his companion, 'I am just too busy for this kind of nonsense. I haven't come a thousand miles to sit and wait while he talks to a porter.' The other replied, 'When the day comes that he stops having time to talk to a porter, on that day I will not have the time to come one mile to see him.'" King said about this anecdote, "When I heard this story, I knew I was being told something I should never forget" (169). The lesson, of course, is that the hallmark of democratic leadership is the ability to listen to and work to empower the "least of these."

After stressing the importance of listening to reciprocal leadership, King offered solutions about addressing the black community's two remaining political weaknesses. King identified them as the imperative to build broader political alliances and the need to become intense political and social activists. It is during King's discussion of these two weaknesses that he mentions the Jewish community's longstanding tradition of political activism. Recall Coles's claim that King holds up the Jew-

ish community as a model of political activism without acknowledging the long-standing political organizing tradition in the black community. However, King's remedy for limited political alliances was to
bypass traditional party politics by embracing a radical democratic politics steeped in organizing new coalitions. He predicted, "The future of
deep structural changes we seek will not be found in the decaying political machines. It lies in new alliances of Negroes, Puerto Ricans, labor, liberals, certain church and middle-class elements" (King 1968b,
158–59) King's use of the word "new" signified the need for a prolifera-
tion of these alliances; he was not suggesting that they did not exist. In
fact, King cited a radical democratic example from New York City as evidence that these alliances can be successful: "It is noteworthy that the
largest single civil rights action ever conducted was the New York school
boycott, when nearly half a million Negroes and Puerto Ricans united in
a demonstration that emptied segregated schools" (159).

   Ultimately, when King called on black Americans to organize their
power and to form alliances with other groups, he was not denying the
long history of organization and radical democratic action in the black
community. Instead, he was merely suggesting that radical democratic
action needed to take hold across all sectors of the black community—
especially among those on the lower end of the socioeconomic ladder.
King (1968b) worried that "Negroes nurture a persisting myth that Jews
of America attained social mobility and status solely because they had
money" (163). Contrary to this misperception, King explained, "Jews
progressed because they possessed a tradition of education combined
with social and political action" (163). Thus, by singling out the Jewish
community King sought to inculcate a belief among black Americans
that, even if penniless, they could still assert themselves by becoming educated and engaging in political and social activism. Having im-
pugned the fallacious accounts about the rise of Jews in America, King
once again held up exemplary models of political action within the
black community: "The many thousands of Negroes who have already
found intellectual growth and spiritual fulfillment on this path know its
creative possibilities. They are not among the legions of the lost, they
are not crushed by the weight of centuries. *Most heartening, among the*

young the spirit of challenge and determination for change is becoming an unquenchable force" (164; emphasis added). Despite the fact that King represented the old guard in the eyes of many youth, he did not resent their unquenchable determination for change. Rather, he continued to hold them up as a source of inspiration and a model of radical democratic efforts within the black community.

To be clear, my point here is not to deny the charges leveled against King for his many shortcomings. Rather, the aim is to show key moments when King sought to cultivate a healthy relationship with his own fallibility, which enabled him to compassionately listen to others. One such moment, I have argued, can be found in the fifth chapter of King's *Where Do We Go from Here* (1968b). I read King as embracing his fallibility, humbly acknowledging his critics, and calling for a course correction. While these may be admirable actions, even King's fiercest critics within the movement were ultimately working toward a similar aim of achieving justice for black Americans. A more difficult challenge to King's cultivation of healthy sensibilities and practices, though, would present itself in the form of the war in Vietnam.

IV

Today King is lauded for his outspokenness on the war in Vietnam. However, like much about his legacy, the truth about his opposition to the war is much more complicated. For instance, even though "Beyond Vietnam: A Time to Break Silence" is widely viewed as King's landmark speech on the war in Vietnam, it was delivered two years after he first spoke out against America's military engagement on the peninsula. After King raised his voice against the war in 1965, he eventually muted his criticisms in response to the overwhelmingly negative reactions he received. King, embarrassed by his timidity, once again publicly confessed his fallibility: "I want you to know that my mind is made up. I backed up a little when I came out in 1965. My name then wouldn't have been written in any book called 'Profiles of Courage'" (as qtd. in Garrow 2004, 564). Thus, as King ascended the famous pulpit of New York's Riverside Church, he was prepared to deliver a speech aimed at getting all

Americans to acknowledge their own fallibility so that they could compassionately listen to others' critiques of themselves and correct their
past outlooks and future actions.

King (1986) began "Beyond Vietnam: A Time to Break Silence" by explaining that his speech had been tailored to all Americans who "bear
the greatest responsibility in ending a conflict that has exacted a heavy
price on both continents" (232). Recall that King argues in his "Sin and
God's Grace" sermon that no members of society can escape societal
sins such as wars—not even the pacifist. According to King, the war in
Vietnam was like a cancer that threatened the health of the entire body
politic. He proclaimed, "If America's soul becomes totally poisoned,
part of the autopsy must read Vietnam. It can never be saved so long as
it destroys the deepest hopes of men the world over" (King 1986, 234).
Therefore, as members of society, King felt that it was necessary for all
Americans to turn inward and to recognize their responsibility for the
sin of the Vietnam War. King was convinced that the inward gaze that
comes along with acknowledging how all Americans are connected to
the evil of the war in Vietnam would then enable them to look outward
with a sense of compassion for others. He offered, "And as I ponder the
madness of Vietnam and search within myself for ways to understand
and respond to compassion my mind goes constantly to the people of
that peninsula" (234–35). Ultimately, King knew "that there will be no
meaningful solution there until some attempt is made to know them
and hear their broken cries" (235).

King (1986) felt that if Americans searched within themselves, then
they would realize that they were engaging in their own form of "messianic faith." He observed, "The [Vietnamese] must see Americans as
strange liberators" (235). Rather than helping to empower the people
of Vietnam, from their perspective, it seemed as if America was intent
on reinstating their colonization. As King's speech progressed, he con-
tinually tried to get his fellow Americans to imagine how the Vietnamese could possibly feel this way. As evidence, he pointed to America's
support for Vietnam's former colonizer, France, as France sought to re-
gain control of its former colony. When the French proved incapable of
recolonizing Vietnam, King reminded the audience that America then

supported a string of dictators who worked to oppress the Vietnamese people. With this political history as the backdrop, King highlighted an ironic image: "All the while the people read our leaflets and received regular promises of peace and democracy—and land reform. Now they languish under our bombs and consider us—not their fellow Vietnamese—the real enemy" (236). Furthermore, King pointed out, "We have destroyed their two most cherished institutions: the family and the village" (236). Thus, the Vietnamese "watch as we poison their water, as we kill a million acres of their crops. They must weep as bulldozers roar through their areas preparing to destroy the precious trees" (236). The destruction, of course, was not just limited to the resources vital to sustaining human life. Nonmilitary civilian lives had also been extinguished as a result of the nation's military efforts. King noted that we had killed millions of innocent civilians and displaced many more.

With King's constant refrain of "we" he was adamant that no American could disentangle himself or herself from the racist war. Therefore, recognition of one's responsibility for the death and destruction of the Vietnamese required that Americans affirm the dignity and worth of all humans; even those they may have previously "othered." He explained, "Perhaps the more difficult but no less necessary task is to speak for those who have been designated as our enemies" (236). King believed that it was necessary for him to give voice to the National Liberation Front (NLF) so that Americans could consider their unique insight into our fallibility. King (1986) asked of his audience: "What must they think of us in America when they realize that we permitted the repression and cruelty of [Premier] Diem which helped to bring them into being as a resistance group in the south? What do they think of our condoning the violence which led to their own taking up of arms?" (236). King concluded, "Surely we must understand their feelings even if we do not condone their actions" (237). With this statement, one sees that King is calling for a form of compassion that would ultimately transcend the prohibitive boundaries of saints and sinners, friends and enemies, whites and blacks, Jews and Samaritans, Americans and Vietnamese. He pleaded, "Here is the true meaning and value of compassion and nonviolence when it helps us to see the enemy's point of view, to hear his questions, to know his assessment of ourselves. For from his view *we may indeed see the basic weaknesses of our own condition,* and if we are mature, we may learn and grow and profit from the wisdom of the brothers who are called the opposition" (237; emphasis added). Consequently, as difficult as it might be, King's theory of political service requires that individuals acknowledge their own fallibility and engage in a form of patient listening to others' views, even—perhaps especially—those we have "othered."

King realized that admitting fallibility and responsibility are not easy tasks. He lamented, "The world now demands a maturity of America that we may not be able to achieve." He goes on to lay out what this maturity required of all Americans: "It demands that we admit that we have been wrong from the beginning of our adventure in Vietnam, that we have been detrimental to the life of the Vietnamese people. The situation is one in which we must be ready to turn sharply from our present ways" (King 1986, 239). King, who cowered in response to his opposition in 1965, wanted to ensure that his audience did not commit the same mistake. Therefore, he promulgated, "The Western arrogance of feeling that it has everything to teach others and nothing to learn from them is not just" (239). Just as he had begun his speech by admitting his own fallibility and correcting his own course of action, he was seeking to cultivate a willingness among his fellow Americans to do the same. He implored: "We are at the moment when our lives must be placed on the line if our nation is to survive its own folly. Every man of humane convictions must decide on the protest that best suits his convictions, but we must all protest" (240).

The manner in which King instructed Americans to protest the war is important to note for at least two reasons. For starters, King allows for people who are differently situated to determine how they will collectively engage in service. For some this could mean conscientiously objecting to the war; for others it might mean joining street protests or writing to members of congress. Secondly, while King believed that protesting unjust practices is a form of service, his radical theory of service meant that Americans would need to dig down to the roots of the injustices in Vietnam, which ultimately meant the restructuring of American society. Without getting to the root causes of America's injustices, King believed that Americans would find themselves "organizing 'clergy and laymen concerned' committees for the next generation" (240).

Delivered exactly a year before he was assassinated, King's speech in opposition to the Vietnam War incorporates all the elements of his theory of political service. As King explained, to get to the root causes of the nation's many injustices, Americans needed to acknowledge "the giant triplets of racism, extreme materialism, and militarism" and consequently undergo a "revolution of values" (240). Thus, King was calling on Americans to transform themselves by acknowledging their fallibility and developing a sense of love and compassion that sought to transform others. He said, "A true revolution of values will soon cause us to question the fairness and justice of many of our past and present policies" (240–41). To cultivate this form of dangerous altruism, King, once again, invoked the biblical parable of the good Samaritan. "On the one hand, we are called to play the Good Samaritan on life's roadside, but that will be only an initial act" (241). Recall that this biblical story is about a man who is left for dead by a gang of robbers on the side of a very dangerous road. In spite of his grave condition, two men passed him by pretending not to notice him. However, the third passerby—a Samaritan—not only stopped but also administered aid and thus transformed the condition of the man in need.

However, as he had in past speeches and sermons, King called this transformation an initial act because service requires more than merely performing a supererogatory act of kindness; it also requires the transformation of structures of injustice. King (1986) expounded, "One day we must come to see that the whole Jericho Road must be transformed so that men and women will not be constantly beaten and robbed as they make their journey on life's highway" (241). Whereas in the original biblical story the Jericho road was the setting for a chance encounter that enabled the Samaritan to *aid* the man in need, in this passage the Jericho road has become the *cause* of the man's need. In other words, King converted the Jericho road into the unjust structures that allow some to travel life's road relatively unencumbered while others are more constrained. To King's mind, the lesson at the heart of the good Samaritan parable is this: "True compassion is more than flinging a coin to a beggar. It comes to see that an edifice which produces beggars needs restructuring" (241).

In concluding this chapter, I want to highlight the convergence of two roads in King's theory of political service. For King, the symbol of a road stems from his configuration of humanity and is meant to convey the interrelatedness of all humans within society. Thus, King (2007) theorizes one road as the social processes that manifest in the "tragedy of collective and social life" (387). All humans must travel on this road as they journey from sin to salvation. However, salvation is never a final destination; rather, it is a continuous road of striving to be better. King theorizes the other road as the social processes that produce structurally unjust outcomes in the lives of all those who travel on it. The road benefits some tremendously, as it is laden with many advantages and privileges for them. While others who travel this road run into many roadblocks, hurdles, and disadvantages.

In the end, though, these two roads are one and the same. Like sin, all humans are connected to the social processes of structural injustice, which produce beggars on the side of Jericho road. Thus, all humans are responsible for seeking salvation in the form of social justice. Given the sinfulness of the human condition, there will never be a moment when a society can claim to have achieved a state of perfect justice—lest they be labeled the "greatest sinner" (King 2007, 386). Consequently, it's imperative that all humans transform themselves into loving beings who care deeply about the plight of those on life's roadside. Seeking to transform the fate of the other—or even their own—they must collectively work to transform the Jericho road into an edifice that represents more just conditions for all. As King (1986) implored, "Now let us begin. Now let us rededicate ourselves to the long and bitter, but beautiful, struggle for a new world. This is the calling of the sons of God, and our brothers wait eagerly for our response" (243).

EPILOGUE
A LEADER TELLS HIS STORY

Finally we agreed that, in spite of the disadvantages and inevitable sacrifices, our *greatest service* could be rendered in our native South. We came to the conclusion that we had something of a moral obligation to return—at least for a few years.
—MARTIN LUTHER KING JR.

I

The purpose of this book is to construct Martin Luther King Jr.'s theory of political service with the hopes that it might serve as a resource for those engaged in contemporary struggles for justice. This book, however, is not meant to be a "how-to" manual. Instead, I have written it with the goal of providing readers with a better understanding of how one of the nation's foremost champions of social justice conceptualized his own life's work and then fomented a revolutionary spirit of political service among his peers. By singling out King's thought for exploration, I, in no way, mean to diminish the contributions of the many other men, women, and children who have sacrificed to make America a more just and democratic society. If anything, it is my hope that my book can bring to the fore King's understanding that the battle for social justice is not about the efforts of a singular figure; rather, it is about the collective action of the masses. Furthermore, I have attempted to discuss his successes and failures in an even-handed manner, without needlessly building him up or tearing him down.

Despite these facts, I know that there is a great danger in writing about a figure who has been mythologized and venerated on a global scale. Personally speaking, there have been many times while working on this project that I have found myself wondering how my own commitment to political service measures up to King's. I have done this even though I know that it is a counterproductive and often paralyzing train of thought. As I mentioned in the introduction, Lester Spence (2015) cautions, "Freezing both King and the Civil Rights Movement demobilizes black communities by creating a historically inaccurate standard, a perfect standard they cannot possibly hope to meet, a perfect standard the people they are being compared to themselves didn't meet" (110). Spence is correct. The goal of studying historical champions of social justice should be to draw inspiration from them, not to become entombed by their legacy. Therefore, I would like to conclude this book by briefly discussing the seemingly banal account King offers about his personal decision to engage in political service. By doing so, my hope is that we can draw inspiration from King's all-too-common struggle to, quite literally, practice what he preached.

||

King, in his first book-length manuscript, *Stride Toward Freedom* (1958), provided insight into the decision-making process that would carry him to Montgomery, Alabama, where he was catapulted to national fame. In his text, King introduced readers to the 1950s version of himself as a graduate student who was finishing up his PhD and weighing his career options. At the time, King went on the job market deciding between either working in a university or becoming a preacher. He was invited to give several job talks, and during one talk he waxed philosophical about the perils facing modern society. Having impressed the search committee, he was offered the job. Like many young philosophers, King continued to develop his critique of modernity. The catch, of course, was that he did not choose to philosophize within the ivy-covered walls of a university or to the north of the Mason-Dixon Line. Instead, at a crossroads in his life, King decided that he could best serve humanity by opting to speak out against the ills of modern society within the stained glass windows of a church in the heart of the Jim Crow South—a decision that has forever changed the way in which American democracy is practiced.

It is only in hindsight that we can label the decision to move south as one of the most crucial choices that King and his newlywed wife, Coretta, made in helping transform the democratic landscape of America. However, it is also important to keep in mind that King was consciously crafting this image of himself. It is telling that the hardback cover of King's (1958) first book reads, "A leader of his people tells The Montgomery Story: Stride Toward Freedom." In this sense, King is purposefully telling a *story* about how he came to be the "leader" of the Montgomery bus boycott. I emphasize the term "story" because as Alasdair MacIntyre (1984) notes, "I can only answer the question 'What am I to do?' if I can answer the prior question 'Of what story or stories do I find myself a part?'" (201). Thus, it is very useful to focus on how it is that King portrayed his role in this story, to gain an understanding of how he personally sought to answer the question "What am I to do?"

Although "de Lawd" was often criticized by his detractors for presenting himself as a self-anointed, messianic figure, in *Stride Toward Freedom* King strikes a much less self-assured chord. In recounting the story of how he ended up in Montgomery, King confessed that initially he and Coretta had been wary about returning to the South, where they had grown up in the throes of segregation. Part of their hesitation was a matter of personal ambitions. Having both attended college in the North they had the chance to take advantage of many opportunities previously denied them in the South. In particular, Coretta was convinced that a northern city would afford her more of an opportunity to pursue her music career than any city in the South. Meanwhile, King (1958), whose childhood experiences under the Jim Crow laws had hardened into an abhorrence of the unjust system, saw his impending career decision as a "chance to escape from the long night of segregation" (21). More important to them both, as future parents they had to consider whether they wanted to provide their children with an upbringing different from their own. This meant a future free of the burdens of legal segregation that they would inevitably endure in the South.

As King recounted his conversations with Coretta, he articulated two competing desires. One set of desires consisted of the ability to pursue their length of life (the first dimension of a complete life) by achieving their personal aspirations and to make a better life for their children. The other desire was to pursue the breadth of life (the second dimension of a complete life) by dedicating themselves to political service. After carefully weighing the options, King recalled the decisive moment thusly, "Finally we agreed that, in spite of the disadvantages and inevitable sacrifices, our *greatest service* could be rendered in our native South. We came to the conclusion that we had something of a moral obligation to return—at least for a few years" (21; emphasis added). While deciding between their competing desires the Kings were engaged in a moment of critical reflection, a process by which they sought to articulate what it was they held most valuable in their lives.

This process of critical reflection is what political theorist Charles Taylor (1985) calls a "strong evaluation." According to Taylor's definition, strong evaluations do not just consider the outcome but also the "quality of our motivations." In other words, in the case of strong evaluations individuals are "concerned with the qualitative worth of different desires" (16). Those who make decisions based solely on preferences are said to be weak evaluators. Weak evaluators, despite possessing a will and having the ability to reflect and evaluate, lack what Taylor calls depth. The issue of depth is important to Taylor for it signals a level of articulacy about our decisions. As he explains, "Strong evaluation is not just a condition of articulacy about preferences, but also about the quality of life, the kind of beings we are or want to become. It is in this sense deeper" (16).

Although Taylor does not believe that a strong evaluation is just about being able to articulate one's preferences, he stresses its importance in the process of a strong evaluation. For, as Taylor notes, our desires are not simply given; instead: "We give it a formulation in words or images. Indeed, by the fact that we are linguistic animals our desires and aspirations cannot but be articulated in one way or another" (36). This is because "articulations," according to Taylor, "are attempts to formulate what is initially inchoate, or confused, or badly formulated. But this kind of formulation and reformulation does not leave its object unchanged. To give a certain articulation is to shape our sense of what we desire or what we hold important in a certain way" (36). Therefore, the process of articulating our desires and values plays a crucial role in molding the beings we wish to become.

For the Kings, undergoing the process of a strong evaluation helped them become more articulate about their desire to return to the South. Upon completion of their strong evaluation they were enabled to claim with confidence that returning to the South to serve others was a far more superior decision than remaining in the comforts of the North. We see how the process of critical reflection helped the Kings reach a new level of depth when King (1958) explained, "The South, after all, was our home. Despite its shortcomings we loved it as home, and had a real desire to do something about the problems that we had felt so keenly as youngsters. We never wanted to be considered detached spectators" (21). Interestingly, the language of detached spectator would become a staple of King's "The American Dream" speeches (see chapter 2) and signaled a lack of commitment to political service. And, just as King had called on black Americans to do in his "The American Dream" speeches over the ensuing years, we get an early glimpse of the Kings articulating their most deeply held values and then taking up their responsibility to make them a reality. Whether in King's personal life or in his public orations, he consistently argued that mere espousal of one's values means nothing if one is not also willing to undertake the actions necessary to bring those values to fruition.

Another consistency between King's public and private life was his emphasis on the need for individuals to transform themselves before they could transform others and structures of injustice. For the Kings this meant transforming their disposition toward living under an oppressive, white power, southern regime. However, according to King's recounting of their decision to move to Montgomery, the process of critical reflection had a profound impact on Coretta's outlook. King observed that even though Coretta initially resisted returning to the racist environment she endured during her formative years, after engaging in critical reflection she "looked at Montgomery with fresh eyes" (23). This is a fascinating transformation given the fact that the South was still governed by Jim Crow laws. Even still, King noted that although the conditions in the South remained unchanged, Coretta had been personally transformed. "And with her sense of optimism and balance ... she placed her faith on the side of the opportunities and the challenges for Christian service that were offered by Dexter and the Montgomery community" (23). Despite Coretta's deep reservations, upon gaining depth about what she truly valued she was able to return to the South and begin the process of transforming others and structures of injustice.

The couple's transformation notwithstanding, King still experienced lapses in confidence and moments when white violence threatened to extinguish his political agency. For instance, as David Garrow (2004) notes, "When the MIA's presidency unexpectedly was thrust upon him on December 5, King was uncertain of his ability to lead a community he had resided in so briefly" (51). To further complicate matters, just as King began to settle into his role as the president of the MIA, he began to receive daily death threats. Surprisingly, King did not portray himself as the gallant leader who was impervious to personal fears and desires to quit. Instead, King revealed his all-too-human impulse to resign from his post while saving face before the public. King (1958) confessed:

> One night toward the end of January I settled into bed late, after a strenuous day. Coretta had already fallen asleep and just as I was about to doze off the telephone rang. An angry voice said, "Listen, nigger, we've taken all we want from you; before next week you'll be sorry you ever came to Montgomery." I hung up, but I couldn't sleep. It seemed that all of my fears had come down on me at once. I had reached the saturation point.
>
> I got out of bed and began to walk the floor. Finally I went to the kitchen and heated a pot of coffee. *I was ready to give up.* With my cup of coffee sitting untouched before me I tried to think of a way to move out of the picture *without appearing a coward.* In this state of exhaustion, *when my courage had all but gone,* I decided to take my problem to God. With my head in my hands, I bowed over the kitchen table and prayed aloud. The words I spoke to God that midnight are still vivid in my memory. "I am here taking a stand for what I believe is right. *But now I am afraid.* The people are looking to me for leadership, and if I stand before them without strength and courage, they too will falter. I am at the end of my

powers. I have nothing left. I've come to the point where I can't face it alone." (134; emphasis added)

When the threat of white racial violence had nearly succeeded in extinguishing King's political agency he pursued the height of life (the third dimension of a complete life) as a resource to sustain him—just as he implored the black community of Birmingham to do, nearly a decade later, in his eulogy for the victims of the 16th Street Baptist Church bombing. Upon concluding his prayer, King recounted, "At that moment I experienced the presence of the Divine as I had never experienced Him before. It seemed as though I could hear the quiet assurance of an inner voice saying: 'Stand up for righteousness, stand up for truth; and God will be at your side forever.' Almost at once my fears began to go. My uncertainty disappeared. I was ready to face anything" (134–35). Drawing on God as his source of sustenance, King was able to face his fears and endure the 381-day boycott of the Montgomery bus line.

However, praying for the strength and courage to carry on in the battle against white oppression was not the only way in which King pursued the height of life during his tenure as a leader in the civil rights movement. In the wake of the bus boycott King became acutely aware of the fact that he was now being heralded as a symbol of the movement. With King's newfound notoriety he became suddenly saddled with lofty and often unobtainable expectations. Thus, King began to undergo another process of critical reflection to ensure that he could represent the movement to the best of his ability. He explained, "When you are aware that you are a symbol, it causes you to search your soul constantly—to go through this job of self-analysis, to see if you live up to the high and noble principles that people surround you with, and to try at all times to keep the gulf between the public self and the private self at a minimum" (King 1998b, 105). King, though, recognized that this cross was too heavy to bear alone. Therefore, he once again turned to God for guidance. He said, "One of the prayers that I prayed to God every day was: 'O God, help me to see myself in my true perspective. Help me, O God, to see that I'm just a symbol of a movement. Help me to see that I'm the victim of what the Germans call a *Zeitgeist* and that something was getting ready to happen in history. And that a boycott would have taken place in Montgomery, Alabama, if I had never come to Alabama." He continued, "Help me to realize that I'm where I am because of the forces of history and because of the fifty thousand Negroes of Alabama who will never get their names in the papers and in the headlines. O God, help me to see that where I stand today, I stand because others helped me to stand there and because the forces of history projected me there'" (105). For King, pursuing the height of life meant having a resource to provide him with sustenance in the battle against white oppression, but it also meant helping him to recognize that all of humanity is configured such that this battle required collective action and therefore exceeded his individual contributions. Ultimately, King's pursuit of the height of life caused him to see that the Montgomery movement was less about him and more about people such as Mary Fair Burks, Jo Ann Robinson, Rosa Parks, Claudette Colvin, E. D. Nixon, and Ralph Abernathy—just to name a few—collectively transforming themselves, others, and structures of injustice.

As we can see, King, when given a platform to tell his own story, was at pains to stress that the Montgomery movement was not about a larger-than-life figure that swept into Alabama and led the black community in their battle against an oppressive white power structure. Instead, King sought to present himself as an individual who initially wanted to pursue the length of life but upon critical reflection with his wife realized that they could only truly flourish by also pursuing the breadth of life. Furthermore, he wanted the public to see that in pursuit of the breadth of life he was often unsure of himself, concerned for his well-being and that of his family, and extremely aware of the fact that he, alone, could never fulfill the lofty expectations set upon his shoulders. In these moments of fear and loathing, King pursued the height of life by drawing on God as a resource to sustain him and to provide him with a proper perspective about his role in the struggle for justice.

When we unfreeze King from those narratives that have transformed him into a mythical creature, we begin to see a far more relatable human being, one whose story is more like yours and mine than the monuments and holiday and Nobel Peace Prize would suggest. Therefore, we should draw inspiration from the banality of King's story rather than sensationalizing it. My point is not to suggest that King did not possess many exceptional qualities. He most certainly did. However, my larger point is that at the end of the day, King could not escape the frailty of the human condition any more than you or I. It is a testament to King's true character that he did not hesitate to pull back the veil and share his story of imperfection with the masses.

III

If we truly want to unfreeze King from a demobilizing narrative, then there is one more story that we should draw on for inspiration. It's a hypothetical story that King shared at the commencement of his final speech, "I See the Promised Land." In an effort to drum up support for black sanitation workers who went on strike in Memphis, Tennessee, King (1986) asked his audience to take a journey with him to the beginning of time. He then imagined standing there beside God, who asks him, "'Martin Luther King, which age would you like to live in?'" (279). In response, King said that he would have mentally traveled through time and peered over some of the most significant moments in the history of human civilization, ranging from ancient Egypt to the signing of the Emancipation Proclamation. After journeying to each dot on King's metaphorical timeline, he told his audience, "But I wouldn't stop there" (280). Instead, he concluded his story by saying to God, "'If you allow me to live just a few years in the second half of the twentieth century, I will be happy'" (280). King readily admitted, "Now that's a strange statement to make, because the world is all messed up. The nation is sick. Trouble is in the land. Confusion is all around" (280). Rather than lament these facts, King drew inspiration from them. He explained, "That's a strange statement. But I know, somehow, that only when it is dark enough, can you see the stars. And I see God working in this period of the twentieth century in a way that men, in some strange way, are responding—something is happening in our world. The masses of people are rising up" (280). Ultimately, King was attempting to convince his audience that there was no period in which they should prefer to live be-

cause, as he explained, "We have been forced to a point where we're going to have to grapple with the problems that men have been trying to
grapple with through history, but the demands didn't force them to do
it" (280). In other words, what made the mid-1960s a great time to live
was an opportunity to engage in humanity's most meaningful political
service.

I conclude with this story because, by King's criteria, we should all
be thrilled to live in our contemporary moment. At this very moment
in history we are tasked with resisting the deleterious effects of global
capitalism and the neoliberal order, preserving and/or restoring American democracy, ending human trafficking and slavery, saving our
planet from climate change, warding off nuclear annihilation, affirming
that black lives matter, and halting sexual assault—just to name a few
of the challenges. This list appears daunting and unachievable. And the
truth of the matter is that we will never achieve all of these objectives in
our lifetime. That, however, is beside the point. What is most important
is that we do our part while traveling on life's road. If we want to truly
honor King's legacy, then we can do so by following his example of engaging in a critical reflection, becoming more articulate about what it
is that we truly value, and then committing to collectively transforming
ourselves, others, and structures of injustice. By doing so, we, too, can
enact change. Perhaps there won't be any statues erected in our honor;
but, if you recall, King didn't want to be remembered by statues nor for
his many awards. Instead, he just wanted to be remembered for serving others. And although we, as individuals, may not get to the promised
land, it is important to remember what King prophesized to his audience at the end of his last speech, "We, as a people will get to the promised land" (286).

Introduction. The Drum Major Instinct

1. He alternatively referred to the triple evils as the giant evils or the evil triplets. They also shifted between racism, poverty, and militarism; racism, materialism, and militarism; and racism, economic exploitation, and militarism.

2. For instance, President Barack Obama and the first family modeled the apolitical conception of the King holiday by celebrating his legacy as volunteers working at soup kitchens and painting murals at local schools. Also, Eddie Glaude (2016) charges that the annual celebration of the King holiday reinforces the "illusion of color-blindness in a country with dramatic racial inequality" (103).

3. Jennifer J. Yanco (2014), similarly, refers to this process as "misremembering."

4. In recent years there have been edited volumes of essays exploring King's political thought (Birt 2012; Shelby and Terry 2018).

Chapter 1. Service as the New Norm of Greatness

1. For more on the international dimensions of King's thought, see chapter 4.

2. For more on King's thoughts about the necessity for black Americans to lead the struggle for justice, see Chappell (2004, 50).

3. For more on this point, see Jackson (2007), especially chapter 10.

4. Dawson (2001) refers to this period in King's development as disillusioned liberalism.

5. Young (2000) makes a similar argument.

6. For a fuller discussion on the imperative of integration, see Anderson (2010).

Chapter 2. The American Dream

1. While James Cone (1991) acknowledges that King invoked the American dream as a means to call black Americans into action, he believes that King primarily invoked the American dream for white audiences. And although he recognizes that King most explicitly invokes the American dream before exclusively black audiences, he doesn't explain how this fits with his claim that King was primarily invoking the American dream for white audiences.

2. Here King is utilizing Abraham Lincoln's reading of the Declaration of Independence. As Garry Wills (1992) notes, "For most people now, the Declaration means what Lincoln told us it means, as a way of correcting the Constitution itself without overthrowing it" (147).

Chapter 3. Life's Final Common Denominator

1. Certainly Lynch had a penchant for hyperbole, but it should be noted that immediately following his speech several black men who were found to be eavesdropping on the event were severely beaten.

2. Branch indicates that King may have had G. A. Gaston, a resident of Birmingham and one of Alabama's wealthiest blacks, in mind when he made these comments.

Chapter 4. A Call to Conscience

1. This is how one with a Southern drawl would pronounce "The Lord."

2. The sermon was delivered circa 1954–60, but the precise date is unknown.

BIBLIOGRAPHY

Allen, Danielle S. 2004. *Talking to Strangers: Anxieties of Citizenship since Brown v. Board of Education*. Chicago: University of Chicago Press.

Anderson, Elizabeth. 2010. *The Imperative of Integration*. Princeton: Princeton University Press.

Arendt, Hannah. 1958. *The Human Condition*. Chicago: University of Chicago Press.

Barber, Benjamin R. 1992. *An Aristocracy of Everyone: The Politics of Education and the Future of America*. New York: Ballantine Books.

Birt, Robert E. 2012. *The Liberatory Thought of Martin Luther King Jr: Critical Essays on the Philosopher King*. Lanham, Md.: Lexington Books.

Blake, John. 2012. "What Did MLK Think about Gay People?" *CNN*, January 16. http://religion.blogs.cnn.com/2012/01/16/what-did-mlk-think-about-gay-people/.

Bogues, Anthony. 2006. "Reflections on African-American Political Thought: The Many Rivers of Freedom." In *A Companion to African American Studies*, edited by Lewis Gordon and Jane Anna Gordon, 417–34. Oxford: Blackwell.

Bonilla-Silva, Eduardo. 2003. *Racism Without Racists: Color-blind Racism and the Persistence of Racial Inequality in the United States*. Lanham, Md.: Rowman & Littlefield.

Boyte, Harry C. 2004. *Everyday Politics: Reconnecting Citizens and Public Life*. Philadelphia: University of Pennsylvania Press.

Branch, Taylor. 1988. *Parting the Waters: America in the King Years, 1954–63*. New York: Simon & Schuster.

———. 1998. *Pillar of Fire: America in the King Years 1963–65*. New York: Simon & Schuster.

Brown, Wendy. 2015. *Undoing the Demos: Neoliberalism's Stealth Revolution*. New York: Zone Books.

Bruyneel, Kevin. 2014. "The King's Body: The Martin Luther King Jr. Memorial and the Politics of Collective Memory." *History and Memory* 26, no. 1: 75–108.

Burrow, Rufus. 2006. *God and Human Dignity: The Personalism, Theology, and Ethics of Martin Luther King, Jr.* Notre Dame: University of Notre Dame Press.

———. 2014. *Martin Luther King, Jr., and the Theology of Resistance.* Jefferson, N.C.: McFarland.

Carby, Hazel. 1992. "Policing the Black Woman's Body in an Urban Context." *Critical Inquiry* 18, no. 4: 738–55.

Carmichael, Stokely, and Charles Hamilton. 1967. *Black Power: The Politics of Liberation in America.* New York: Random House, 1967.

Carson, Clayborne. 2005. "Between Contending Forces: Martin Luther King, Jr., and the African American Freedom Struggle." *OAH Magazine of History* 19, no. 1: 17–21.

Carter, Dan T. 1995. *The Politics of Rage: George Wallace, the Origins of the New Conservatism, and the Transformation of American Politics.* New York: Simon & Schuster.

Chappell, David L. 2004. *Stone of Hope: Prophetic Religion and the Death of Jim Crow.* Chapel Hill: University of North Carolina Press.

Coates, Ta-Nehisi. 2015. *Between the World and Me.* New York: Spiegel and Grau.

Cohen, Cathy. 1999. *The Boundaries of Blackness: AIDS and the Breakdown of Black Politics.* Chicago: University of Chicago Press.

Coles, Romand. 2008. "Awakening to the Call of Receptive Democratic Progress." *The Good Society* 17, no. 1: 43–51.

Cone, James H. 1991. *Martin & Malcolm & America: A Dream or a Nightmare?* Maryknoll, N.Y.: Orbis Books.

Cullen, Jim. 2003. *The American Dream: A Short History of an Idea that Shaped a Nation.* New York: Oxford University Press.

Dawson, Michael C. 2001. *Black Visions: The Roots of Contemporary African-American Political Ideologies.* Chicago: University of Chicago Press.

Dawson, Michael C., and Megan Ming Francis. 2016. "Black Politics and the Neoliberal Racial Order." *Public Culture* 28, no. 1: 23–62.

Dovidio, John F., and Samuel L. Gaertner. 1986. "The Aversive Form of Racism." In *Prejudice, Discrimination, and Racism*, edited by John F. Dovidio and Samuel L. Gaertner, 61–89. San Diego: Academic Press.

Du Bois, W. E. B. 1903. *The Souls of Black Folk.* Chicago: A.C. McClurg & Company.

Dyson, Michael Eric. 2000. *I May Not Get there with You: The True Martin Luther King, Jr.* New York: Free Press.

Fairclough, Adam. 1987. *To Redeem the Soul of America: The Southern Christian Leadership Conference and Martin Luther King, Jr.* Athens: University of Georgia Press.

Garrow, David J. 2004. *Bearing the Cross: Martin Luther King, Jr., and the Southern Christian Leadership Conference.* New York: Perennial Classics.

Glaude, Eddie. 2016. *Democracy in Black: How Race Still Enslaves the American Soul.* New York: Broadway Books.

Hanson, Sandra L., and John Zogby. 2010. "The Polls–Trends Attitudes About The American Dream." *Public Opinion Quarterly* 74, no. 3: 570–84.

Harding, Vincent. 1996. *Martin Luther King: The Inconvenient Hero*. Maryknoll, N.Y.: Orbis Books.

Harvey, David. 2005. *A Brief History of Neoliberalism*. Oxford: Oxford University Press.

Hauerwas, Stanley, and Romand Coles. 2008. *Christianity, Democracy, and the Radical Ordinary: Conversations between a Radical Democrat and a Christian*. Eugene, Ore.: Cascade Books.

Higginbotham, Evelyn Brooks. 1993. *Righteous Discontent: The Women's Movement in the Black Baptist Church, 1880–1920*. Cambridge: Harvard University Press.

Hochschild, Jennifer L. 1995. *Facing Up to the American Dream: Race, Class and the Soul of the Nation*. Princeton: Princeton University Press.

Holmes, Jack. 2018. "Martin Luther King, Jr. Spreads the Gospel of Four-Wheel Drive." *Esquire*, February 5. www.esquire.com/news-politics/a16569990 /dodge-martin-luther-king-commercial-mlk/.

Howard-Pitney, David. 2005. *The African American Jeremiad: Appeals for Justice in America*. Philadelphia: Temple University Press.

Ivory, Luther D. 1997. *Toward a Theology of Radical Involvement: The Theological Legacy of Martin Luther King Jr*. Nashville: Abingdon Press.

Jackson, Thomas F. 2007. *From Civil Rights to Human Rights: Martin Luther King and the Struggle for Economic Justice*. Philadelphia: University of Pennsylvania Press.

Kelley, Robin D. G. 2002. *Freedom Dreams: The Black Radical Imagination*. Boston: Beacon Press.

Kertzer, David I. 1988. *Ritual, Politics, and Power*. New Haven: Yale University Press.

King, Martin Luther. 1958. *Stride Toward Freedom: The Montgomery Story*. New York: Harper and Row.

———. 1965. "Remaining Awake through a Great Revolution" (speech). In "Martin Luther King, Jr. at Oberlin." *Electronic Oberlin Group*, http://www2 .oberlin.edu/external/EOG/BlackHistoryMonth/MLK/CommAddress.html, accessed May 2018.

———. 1967a. "The Three Evils of Society" (speech delivered at the National Conference on New Politics, 31 August 1967). *Scribd*, www.scribd.com /doc/134362247/Martin-Luther-King-Jr-The-Three-Evils-of-Society-1967, accessed May 2018.

———. 1967b. "A Christmas Sermon" (sermon delivered 24 December 1967). *The King Center*, http://thekingcenter.org/archive/document/christmas -sermon#, accessed May 2018.

———. 1968a. "A New Sense of Direction" (speech delivered to the Southern Christian Leadership Conference, 4 April 1968). *Carnegie Counsel*, www .carnegiecouncil.org/publications/articles_papers_reports/4960, accessed May 2018.

———. 1968b. *Where Do We Go from Here: Chaos or Community?* Boston: Beacon Press.

———. 1986. *A Testament of Hope: The Essential Writings and Speeches of Martin Luther King, Jr.* Edited by James M. Washington. San Francisco: Harper & Row.

———. 1998a. *A Knock at Midnight: Inspiration from the Great Sermons of Reverend Martin Luther King, Jr.* Edited by Clayborne Carson and Peter Holloran. New York: Intellectual Properties Management in association with Warner Books.

———. 2001. *A Call to Conscience: The Landmark Speeches of Dr. Martin Luther King, Jr.* Edited by Clayborne Carson, and Kris Shepard. New York: Intellectual Properties Management in association with Warner Books.

———. 2005. *The Papers of Martin Luther King, Jr. Volume V.* Edited by Clayborne Carson, Tenisha Armstrong, Susan Carson, Adrienne Clay, and Kieran Taylor. Berkeley: University of California Press.

———. 2007. *The Papers of Martin Luther King, Jr. Volume VI.* Edited by Clayborne Carson, Susan Carson, Susan Englander, Troy Jackson, and Gerald L. Smith. Berkeley: University of California Press.

———. 2010. *Strength to Love.* Minneapolis: Fortress Press. King, Martin Luther, and Clayborne Carson. 1998b. *The Autobiography of Martin Luther King, Jr.* New York: Warner Books.

MacIntyre, Alasdair C. 1984. *After Virtue: A Study in Moral Theory.* Notre Dame: University of Notre Dame Press.

Malcolm X. 1965. *Malcolm X Speaks: Selected Speeches and Statements.* Edited by George Breitman. New York: Grove Press.

Marsh, Charles. 2005. *The Beloved Community: How Faith Shapes Social Justice, from the Civil Rights Movement to Today.* New York: Basic Books.

McWhorter, Diane. 2001. *Carry Me Home: Birmingham, Alabama: The Climactic Battle of the Civil Rights Revolution.* New York: Simon & Schuster.

Myrdal, Gunnar. 1944. *An American Dilemma: The Negro Problem and Modern Democracy.* New York: Harper & Row.

Niebuhr, Reinhold. 1932. *Moral Man and Immoral Society: A Study in Ethics and Politics.* New York: Scribner.

Obama, Barack. 2013. "FULL TRANSCRIPT: President Obama's Speech on the 50th Anniversary of the March on Washington." *The Washington Post*, 28 August. www.washingtonpost.com/politics/transcript-president-obamas-speech-on-the-50th-anniversary-of-the-march-on-washington/2013/08/28/0138e01e offb-11e3-8cdd-bcdc09410972_story.html?utm_term=.9d124c8a18eb, accessed May 2018.

Olson, Joel. 2004. *The Abolition of White Democracy.* Minneapolis: University of Minnesota Press.

Payne, Charles. 1989. "Ella Baker and Models of Social Change." *Signs* 14, no. 4: 885–99.

Ralph, James R. 1993. *Northern Protest: Martin Luther King, Jr., Chicago, and the Civil Rights Movement.* Cambridge: Harvard University Press.

Ransby, Barbara. 2003. *Ella Baker and the Black Freedom Movement*. Chapel Hill: University of North Carolina Press.

Robinson, Cedric J. 1983. *Black Marxism: The Making of the Black Radical Tradition*. London: Zed Press.

Rogers, Melvin. 2015. "What Ta-Nehisi Coates Is Missing." *Dissent Magazine*, July 31. www.dissentmagazine.org/online_articles/between-world-me-ta-nehisi-coates-review-despair-hope, accessed May 2018.

Shelby, Tommie, and Brandon M. Terry, eds. 2018. *To Shape a New World: Essays on the Political Philosophy of Martin Luther King, Jr*. Cambridge: Belknap.

Shulman, George M. 2008. *American Prophecy: Race and Redemption in American Political Culture*. Minneapolis: University of Minnesota Press.

Singh, Nikhil P. 2004. *Black Is a Country: Race and the Unfinished Struggle for Democracy*. Cambridge: Harvard University Press.

Sitkoff, Harvard. 2008. *King: Pilgrimage to the Mountaintop*. New York: Hill and Wang.

Spence, Lester K. 2015. *Knocking the Hustle: Against the Neoliberal Turn in Black Politics*. Brooklyn, N.Y.: Punctum Books.

Sundquist, Eric J. 2009. *King's Dream*. New Haven: Yale University Press.

Taylor, Charles. 1985. *Philosophical Papers: Volume 1*. Cambridge: Cambridge University Press.

Taylor, Keeanga-Yamahtta. 2016. *From #blacklivesmatter to Black Liberation*. Chicago: Haymarket Books.

The Official MLK Day of Service Site. 2013. http://mlkday.gov/about/serve-onkingday.php, accessed 12 November 2013.

Wade, Wyn C. 1987. *The Fiery Cross: The Ku Klux Klan in America*. New York: Simon & Schuster.

Weingarten, Gene, and Michael E. Ruane. 2011. "Maya Angelou Says King Memorial Inscription Makes Him Look 'Arrogant.'" *The Washington Post*, August 30. http://articles.washingtonpost.com/2011-08-30/local/35272106_1_peace-and-righteousness-inscription-lei-yixin.

West, Cornel. 2015. Introduction to *The Radical King*, by Martin Luther King Jr., edited by Cornel West. Boston: Beacon Press.

———. 2017. "Ta-Nehisi Coates Is the Neoliberal Face of the Black Freedom Struggle." *The Guardian*, December 17. www.theguardian.com/commenisfree/2017/dec/17/ta-nehisi-coates-neoliberal-black-struggle-cornel-west, accessed May 2018.

Wills, Garry. 1992. *Lincoln at Gettysburg*. New York: Simon & Schuster. Wills, Richard W. 2011. *Martin Luther King, Jr. and the Image of God*. New York: Oxford University Press.

Yanco, Jennifer J. 2014. *Misremembering Dr. King: Revisiting the Legacy of Martin Luther King Jr*. Bloomington: Indiana University Press.

Young, Iris Marion. 2000. *Inclusion and Democracy*. Oxford: Oxford University Press.

———. 2011. *Responsibility for Justice*. Oxford: Oxford University Press.

9 780820 355542